MARATHON TRAINING

SECOND EDITION

JOE HENDERSON

HUMAN KINETICS

Library of Congress Cataloging-in-Publication Data

Henderson, Joe, 1943-
    Marathon training / Joe Henderson.-- 2nd ed.
        p. cm.
    Includes index.
    ISBN 0-7360-5191-0 (Soft cover)
    1. Marathon running--Training. I. Title.
    GV1065.17.T73H45 2004
    796.42'52--dc22   2003017695

ISBN-10: 0-7360-5191-0
ISBN-13: 978-0-7360-5191-0

The Web addresses cited in this text were current as of October 2003.

Acquisitions Editor: Martin Barnard; **Developmental Editor:** Leigh LaHood; **Copyeditor:** Jan Feeney; **Proofreader:** Annette Pierce; **Indexer:** Betty Frizzéll; **Graphic Designer:** Fred Starbird; **Graphic Artist:** Kim McFarland; **Photo Manager:** Dan Wendt; **Cover Designer:** Jack W. Davis; **Photographer (cover):** Bongarts/SportsChrome; **Photographers (interior):** Photos on pages ix and 160 © Acestock; photos on pages xi, xx, 16, 96, 144, and 208 © Sport the Library; photos on pages 32, 48, 64, and 128 by davidsandersphotos.com; photos on pages 80 and 112 © Richard B. Levine; photo on page 176 © Francis M. Roberts; photos on pages 192 and 214 © Kirk Schlea/Bruce Coleman, Inc.; **Printer:** United Graphics

Human Kinetics books are available at special discounts for bulk purchase. Special editions or book excerpts can also be created to specification. For details, contact the Special Sales Manager at Human Kinetics.

Printed in the United States of America   10 9 8 7 6 5 4 3

Human Kinetics
Web site: www.HumanKinetics.com

United States: Human Kinetics
P.O. Box 5076
Champaign, IL 61825-5076
800-747-4457
e-mail: humank@hkusa.com

Canada: Human Kinetics
475 Devonshire Road, Unit 100
Windsor, ON N8Y 2L5
800-465-7301 (in Canada only)
e-mail: info@hkcanada.com

Europe: Human Kinetics
107 Bradford Road
Stanningley
Leeds LS28 6AT, United Kingdom
+44 (0)113 255 5665
e-mail: hk@hkeurope.com

Australia: Human Kinetics
57A Price Avenue
Lower Mitcham, South Australia 5062
08 8372 0999
e-mail: info@hkaustralia.com

New Zealand: Human Kinetics
Division of Sports Distributors NZ Ltd.
P.O. Box 300 226 Albany
North Shore City, Auckland
0064 9 448 1207
e-mail: info@humankinetics.co.nz

To the Kelleys, John A. the elder, and John J. the younger,
for first inspiring me to try a marathon—
and for being there at my first one in Boston, 1967.

CONTENTS

PREFACE

I've led three lives as a marathoner. Each happened to fall into a distinct period in the event's modern history, featuring a different set of attitudes and approaches.

Marathon Life One took me from 1967 to 1980. Most runners of that time—which in the latter part of that period came to be called the "Running Boom," and in hindsight the "*First* Boom"—were like me: young, fairly fast (at least by today's standards), and male. Women hadn't yet arrived in great numbers, few runners had become longtimers or oldtimers, and the Holy Grails of marathoning were breaking three hours and qualifying for Boston.

Foot and leg miseries, caused by the quest for speed, limited me to shorter races for most of the 1980s. On my return for Marathon Life Two, I found a different event than the one I'd left almost a decade earlier. It was bigger, both in numbers of runners and races, and more varied—notably with more women running. Surviving the distance had become more important than beating the clock to most of the new runners and to an older returnee like me.

Health problems unrelated to marathons, or to running in general, ended Marathon Life Two for me in 1995. During the extended break that followed, I wrote and Human Kinetics published my book *Marathon Training*. It was in print for more than a year by the time I returned to running this distance.

Marathon Life Three began for me in 1998. Again I saw changes. In just three years the number of annual marathon finishers in the United States had jumped by more than 100,000. The number of races had climbed by about 100. Organized training groups, often charity fund-raising efforts, had proliferated. Walk-breaking runners and pure walkers had boosted the size of fields and slowed their median times.

My Marathon Life Three coincided with what came to be called the "Second Running Boom." Its runners and run-walkers (of which I'm one) had changed the event so much that they'd updated my thinking on what it means to be a marathoner. The next logical move, then, was to update the book *Marathon Training*. The most obvious makeover is in the photos. The look of marathoning has changed since the mid-1990s. Here we not only update the styles of clothing and shoes but also better reflect the larger and more diverse makeup of current race fields. For instance, the first *Marathon Training* cover pictured four young men racing at the front. Although we continue to honor such runners, they don't accurately represent today's typical marathoner—which is why our new cover looks so much different than the original.

The first book carried the subtitle *The Proven 100-Day Program for Success*. I assumed then that runners were reasonably well trained before this three-month training period began—that they already had been running for a year or more, that they could run at least an hour at a time, and that they'd completed at least a 10K race and ideally a half-marathon. We can't make such assumptions anymore. Many people now make the marathon their first running goal. They may start from the couch and resolve to finish a marathon within their first year—often making it their first race of any length. For them I've added advice on the prerequisites of marathon training, or how they must pretrain *before* the 100-day countdown begins.

Each thought for the day, a brief essay that accompanies each day of this program, is entirely new in this book. Again, each essay reflects the changes in thinking, trends, and techniques of marathoning since the book's first publication in 1997.

Each training tip, a one-paragraph daily lesson for each day of the program, appears here nearly unchanged. So do the training programs. These schedules and supporting tips were 30 years in the making before the original book came out, and they need little editing now.

As in the previous edition, this book gives you choices—of how seriously you want to take the marathon; exactly what distances and paces you intend to run; and on which days you plan to run long, run fast, run easily, or rest. You know best what you're trying to accomplish and how the pieces of this puzzle will fit together for you.

I took the book this far. Now it's up to you to finish it by writing your own marathon-training story. May it have a happy ending.

INTRODUCTION: OUR MARATHONS

I am a marathoner—never a fast one and never a contender for any prize, but none of that really matters. The marathon is less a race for records and prizes than it is a survival test that rewards all who finish. I've survived dozens of these events.

Like everyone who has ever run a marathon, I have a story to tell. Before advising you on how to write a much more important story—your own—allow me to relate my small tale. It reflects my feelings about this marvelous event as a whole and how I arrived at giving advice on training for it.

I love marathoning as a sport, and love no single marathon more than Boston. That's partly because it is the ancestral home of marathoning in the United States, but especially because it was my birthplace as a marathoner. Boston 1967 was my first try at this distance.

A first marathon is like a first love. You might bumble through it, but you never forget it. Nothing you do later will ever be quite as memorable as your initiation, even if its memories are painful. Mine aren't. My first marathon wasn't the fiasco that I'd heard was the birthright of first-timers. It was perfect. Perfect in training (an accidentally ideal mix of long runs, fast runs, and rest) and perfect in execution. (What Heartbreak Hill? What 20-mile wall?) It was too perfect to show what marathoning really is.

Maybe I should have stopped with the first one. It would have given me a perfect career: a surprisingly good time and an amazingly trouble-free run in the most historic of marathons. But that isn't how love works. You taste it once and want more. You go for more, and reality sets in.

Boston's course and conditions are record makers and record spoilers, with the weather there either helping or hurting times. I ran my coldest and hottest marathons there, which were also my fastest and slowest (at that stage). The early downhill miles at Boston either produce a fast finish or wreck it with a too-fast start, as demonstrated one year when I combined my best first half and worst second half.

I never would better that first Boston time. No marathon would ever go as smoothly as that one did. But I've come back to the marathon nearly four dozen times. You don't dump an old and deep love after inevitably seeing the imperfections.

Multiply my memories by the tens of thousands of people who have ever run at Boston, and the hundreds of thousands who've run other marathons, and you begin to understand our collective love affair with this event. The marathon celebrated a double centennial as the first edition of this book went

You're one among thousands of marathon runners, but realize also that you're doing what 999 people in 1,000 couldn't do.

to press. The marathon as a race (as opposed to a tale from Greek mythology) was born at the first modern Olympics in Athens 1896. The oldest annual marathon, Boston, marked its 100th running in 1996.

Throughout its first century, the marathon stood as a centerpiece of the Olympics. It served as a yearly rite of spring in Boston all that time. But until recently, the race attracted little attention anywhere else. Then came the running boom of the 1970s and 1980s, first in the United States and then around the world. The marathon grew up, exploding in both number of races and size of their fields. Every city of size conducted a marathon of its own—with London, New York City, Honolulu, and Los Angeles attracting fields of 20,000 or more.

Marathons changed in character as well as in size. Up front the leaders ran for prize money. Farther back in the field came runners old and young, male and female, fairly fast and very slow. The event welcomed them all. For most marathoners this wasn't a race but a survival test. Surviving became a form of winning—just as noble in its own way as finishing first and setting records. This attitude helps explain the still-growing appeal of the marathon. In the event's second century about 300,000 marathoners now go this distance each year in the United States alone. This is triple the number from 20 years earlier.

The marathon, which is about enduring and surviving, has endured and survived. By running one, you become part of a long and proud history. You join a parade of marathoners that reaches from the 19th century into the 21st.

But enough rhapsodizing. Let's get down to the realities of running a marathon. No matter how many people finish marathons, getting to the starting line is an individual sport. No one else can do the training for you, and no one can run a good marathon without training.

TRAINING COMMITMENT

The thought of covering 26.2 miles, or 42.2 kilometers, on foot is as frightening as it is fascinating. The act itself might appear as simple as putting one foot in front of the other and remembering to alternate feet. But doing this for hours on end can seriously test your physical as well as mental resources.

A marathon takes anywhere from a little over two hours to a lot more than five hours to complete. The event drains your fluid and fuel reserves. It hammers your feet and legs. It makes you wonder at some point late in the race, "What am I doing here?"

What happens during the marathon is neither the beginning nor the end of your efforts. You've invested several months of training into getting there, and you'll spend another month or more getting over this effort.

So you see that the decision to run a marathon is not made lightly. It's a major commitment of time and energy. This training can be quite gratifying if done right, or equally distressing if done wrong.

In this book we try to maximize gratification and minimize distress. But I won't mislead you: There is no easy, risk-free way to run a marathon. If there were, everyone would do it and you wouldn't feel so special. Although it's

Your big challenge is getting to the marathon starting line fit and healthy.

true that hundreds of thousands of people are marathoners, they still represent only about 1 in 10 people who enter races, 1 in 100 who run at all, and 1 in 1,000 from the general population.

You don't choose to run a marathon *despite* its difficulty but *because* of its difficulty. You like the feeling of aiming for a distant goal that not just anyone would tackle—and eventually reaching it.

You can't fake a marathon. Maybe you can wake up one fine spring morning and decide to run a 5K or 10K race that day, trusting your normal few miles of running to carry you through. Try this in a marathon, and the distance will quickly reveal your inadequacies. This event requires special train-ing—and lots of it for a long time. Here we focus on those training requirements. This isn't primar-ily a book about the history or personalities or statistics of the marathon or about training for any other distance but the mara-thon. This certainly isn't a primer on running in general, since you must have learned the basics elsewhere before picking up this book. It deals almost exclusively with how to get to and through a race that justifies all the time and effort you put into it.

I've been following marathon-training programs since the 1960s and writing them for other runners since the 1970s. My first published schedule appeared in a 1977 issue of *Runner's World*. That short article, written in haste, drew more response than all my previous stories combined. Hundreds of marathoners told me of their experiences, positive and otherwise. I've talked with thousands more runners since then at marathon-training clinics and at races throughout the United States and Canada and at the college running classes that I teach. These runners too have let me know what worked—and what didn't.

The programs in this book are only distant cousins of those I might have circulated half a lifetime ago. The change results partly from runners' feedback and partly from influential experimenters such as Tom Osler (who introduced walking breaks to marathoning) and Jeff Galloway (who inspired a whole new way of looking at marathoning).

But marathon programs have changed mostly because of the changes in marathoners in recent decades. Never in the long history of this event has the gap between the fastest and slowest finishers been wider. The median time—equal numbers faster and slower—is now double the winner's time. The late arrivals take three or more times as long to complete the course as the leaders do.

People enter marathons for many different reasons: to finish any way they can (running, walking, or some mix thereof), to run every step, to cover the distance faster than they've done it before, to qualify for Boston, to win an age-group prize or an overall award. We address all of the reasons here. We ignore runners training to reach the Olympic Trials or win some cash. They don't need a book written by a runner who rarely came within an hour of their times.

TRAINING GOALS

Here we split marathoners into three groups. The group you join, and the training program you choose, depends on your experience and goals. We call these groups Cruisers, Pacers, and Racers.

• Cruisers aim primarily to finish, and final time doesn't concern them much (as long as they beat the deadline for closing the course). They enhance their chances of finishing by inserting walking breaks—a technique that noted running author Galloway calls "cruising." I recommend that most first-timers and all low-key marathoners follow the Cruiser training program.

• Pacers aim for time goals, or in runners' terms try to set personal records (PRs). They typically try to run the entire distance, without planned walking breaks, to maintain their chosen pace. I recommend that runners select the Pacer training program only after cruising their first marathon. As an exception, runners without marathon experience but with an extensive background in short-distance racing can jump directly into Pacer training.

• Racers aim to compete with other marathoners. They race for prizes in their age division or overall. They earn these honors with the hardest training this book has to offer. I recommend the Racer program only to runners whose run-for-time effort in a previous marathon placed them within sight of the people they want to beat.

The lines between the groupings are more blurry than they sound here. You might be a Cruising Pacer or a Pacing Racer who adjusts training to fit this blending of goals. Or you might be a Cruiser in your first race, then graduate to Pacing and even to Racing in later marathons. The training plans are flexible enough to accommodate the whole range of ambitions.

Before you start training for your first or fastest or simply next marathon, choose a race. You face a world of choices, because nearly every country has a marathon, and most states and Canadian provinces have several. You can find a marathon somewhere any weekend of the year. (See a list of more than 100 in the back of this book.) Your choice of marathon will depend on factors such as the ease and expense of travel, the time of year, the expected weather and the difficulty of the course, as well as the history of the race and the perks it offers.

Once you've picked a marathon, enter it early. This will seal your commitment to train for it. By knowing exactly where you're going, you also can prepare better. You can study the course map and run parts of it if you live nearby or mimic its terrain if you don't.

Once you know the race date, count backward by 13 weeks—or 91 days, to be exact. This is where your training begins. The programs here actually last 100 days, with the final ones covering the vital early recovery period after the marathon.

TRAINING PLANS

Now select the training plan that best suits you: Cruiser, Pacer, or Racer. Note that each program has prerequisites that you'll need to meet before you can enter the 100-day plan (see the table at the bottom of this page).

• Cruisers: You should have taken a recent nonstop run of 6 miles (10K) or more, done a run-walk of at least 10 miles (16K), and finished a race of any distance. Don't make the marathon the first organized event that you've ever entered.

• Pacers: You should be able to run 10 miles (16K) nonstop currently, have raced at least the half-marathon distance in the past and, in most cases, have "cruised" a previous marathon. Before you can start breaking personal records, you must set the original one.

• Racers: You should have "paced" a previous nonstop marathon and currently be running at least 10 miles (16K) comfortably. You're a hardened veteran of shorter-distance races.

PRETRAINING NEEDS

Before you begin any of the marathon training programs outlined in this book, I strongly advise you to complete the following prerequisites.

	Longest recent run	Race experience
Cruisers	6 miles (10K) nonstop; 10 miles (16K) with walk breaks	10K finish; half-marathon optional but recommended
Pacers	10 miles (16K)	Half-marathon finish; Cruiser marathon optional but recommended
Racers	10 miles (16K)	Marathon finish with at least Pacer emphasis

All three programs contain similar ingredients. The quantities (and, of course, the speeds) vary.

1. Big day: One a week for most runners. The long run is most important because it most closely resembles the marathon itself, but it isn't the only option. Other choices are a semilong run at half the distance of the most recent long one, a fast run of short distance (up to 3 miles or 5K), or a race of up to 10K.

2. Other training days: The several easy days between big days. Here you run by time periods for unknown distance, which helps remove the temptation to "race" these runs that are meant to be relaxed. They last 30 to 60 minutes.

3. Rest days: At least one and as many as three scheduled each week. Cross-training is allowed—in fact, encouraged—on these days. But the effort of swimming, hiking, or walking should be less taxing than an easy run.

The ingredients are simple, and the day-by-day scheduling is flexible. You make the final decision on which day to run what, choosing from a range of distances. This gives you plenty of wiggle room to set your own pace, to time your runs or go untimed (or to wear a heart-rate monitor), to run on or off roads, to run hills or flats, to run with companions or alone, or to rest or run easily or cross-train.

These programs also let you fit the training into your family and job routines and to adjust for minor physical glitches. The accompanying tables list specific recommendations for each of the three training plans and the suggested weekly runs in each program.

TRAINING QUESTIONS

No matter how long this introductory section might have run, it still would have raised questions in marathoners' minds. Here I anticipate 10 of them:

1. "What if I've already run longer than the starting distance listed here?" Start later in the program, about 2 miles (or 3K) above your recent peak. This lets you either shorten the program's length or progress more slowly than what's recommended here.

2. "How quickly do I advance in distance of the long run?" No more than 2 miles (3K) per run. This averages less than 10 percent per week (though you aren't asked to run long weekly) for the life of the program. This is a widely recommended limit on increasing distances.

3. "How often do I run each long distance?" Only once. This gives you a necessary sense of steady progress instead of the feeling that you've already done this.

TRAINING PLANS

	Cruisers	Pacers	Racers
Runs per week	4 or 5, including 1 big day	5 or 6, including 1 big day	6 days each week, including 2 big days
Long runs	Every 3rd week, longest 18 to 20 miles (29 to 32K)	Every 2 to 3 weeks, longest 20 to 22 miles (32 to 35K)	2 out of 3 weeks, longest 22 to 24 miles (35 to 38K)
Semilong runs	Every 3rd week, longest 9 to 10 miles (15 to 16K)	Every 2 to 4 weeks, longest 10 to 11 miles (16 to 18K)	Every 3rd week, longest 11 to 12 miles (18 to 19K)
Fast runs or race	Every 3rd week, 5K or less	Every 3 or 4 weeks, 5K to 10K	Once each week, 1 mile (1.6K) to 10K
Easy runs	3 or 4 days a week, 30 to 45 minutes	4 or 5 days a week, 30 to 60 minutes	4 days a week, 30 to 60 minutes
Rest days	2 or 3 a week, cross-training optional but never a hard effort	1 or 2 a week, cross-training optional but never a hard effort	1 a week, cross-training optional but never a hard effort

4. "What do I do if I miss a scheduled long run?" Try not to miss it altogether. It's the most important part of the program. Run it in place of the next semilong or fast run on your schedule.

5. "How do I check distances on unfamiliar courses?" If you can't measure them, simply run by time periods. Convert the training distance at your usual pace to hours and minutes and run for that length of time.

6. "How fast do I go on the long ones—my predicted marathon pace?" Nowhere close. Focus on extending your distances, which is best done at about 1 minute per mile (35 seconds per kilometer) slower than you could race that distance. Train for speed on other weekends.

7. "How do I take walk breaks?" Early, brief, and often. They work best when taken from the start, for about one minute at a time, and at the rate of once per mile or kilometer.

8. "How much distance should I total each week in training?" Don't count weekly miles or kilometers. This can cause you to run too much on days that should be easy (or off), and it can leave you tired for the ones that count.

9. "What if the worst happens and I complete the training but miss the marathon?" Have a backup race in mind, one near the date of your original target. Don't let the effort go to waste.

CRUISERS			
Week	**Big day**	**Other runs**	**Rest days**
1	12 to 14 miles (20 to 22K)	3 or 4 of 30 to 45 minutes	2 or 3 off or easy "cross"
2	6 to 7 miles (10 to 11K)	3 or 4 of 30 to 45 minutes	2 or 3 off or easy "cross"
3	5K race or fast training	3 or 4 of 30 to 45 minutes	2 or 3 off or easy "cross"
4	14 to 16 miles (22 to 25K)	3 or 4 of 30 to 45 minutes	2 or 3 off or easy "cross"
5	7 to 8 miles (11 to 13K)	3 or 4 of 30 to 45 minutes	2 or 3 off or easy "cross"
6	5K race or fast training	3 or 4 of 30 to 45 minutes	2 or 3 off or easy "cross"
7	16 to 18 miles (26 to 29K)	3 or 4 of 30 to 45 minutes	2 or 3 off or easy "cross"
8	8 to 9 miles (13 to 15K)	3 or 4 of 30 to 45 minutes	2 or 3 off or easy "cross"
9	5K race or fast training	3 or 4 of 30 to 45 minutes	2 or 3 off or easy "cross"
10	18 to 20 miles (29 to 32K)	3 or 4 of 30 to 45 minutes	2 or 3 off or easy "cross"
11	9 to 10 miles (15 to 16K)	3 or 4 of 30 to 45 minutes	2 or 3 off or easy "cross"
12	1 hour	3 or 4 of 30 to 45 minutes	2 or 3 off or easy "cross"
13	None	3 or 4 of about 30 minutes	3 or 4 off or easy "cross"
14	Marathon race	None	1 off
15	None	3 or 4 short and easy	3 or 4 off or easy "cross"

10. "How soon can I run my next marathon after finishing this one?" How does six months later sound? You could run another one much sooner, but two per year is a reasonable limit. For half the year you can do something other than train for and recover from marathons.

TRAINING RECORDS

This book is arranged to be read one day at a time, just as you train. Each of the 100 days includes a thought for the day and a training tip from me.

The thought for the day is general advice and observations on running, and this essay often continues from one day to the next. The one-paragraph training tip fits a specific theme for the week. Together these items cover a variety of topics, giving you information and inspiration that help you complete the training—and eventually the marathon itself.

Week	Big day	Other runs	Rest days
1	12 to 14 miles (20 to 22K)	4 or 5 of 30 to 60 minutes	1 or 2 off or easy "cross"
2	6 to 7 miles (10 to 11K)	4 or 5 of 30 to 60 minutes	1 or 2 off or easy "cross"
3	14 to 16 miles (22 to 25K)	4 or 5 of 30 to 60 minutes	1 or 2 off or easy "cross"
4	5K to 10K race or fast training	4 or 5 of 30 to 60 minutes	1 or 2 off or easy "cross"
5	16 to 18 miles (26 to 29K)	4 or 5 of 30 to 60 minutes	1 or 2 off or easy "cross"
6	8 to 9 miles (13 to 15K)	4 or 5 of 30 to 60 minutes	1 or 2 off or easy "cross"
7	18 to 20 miles (29 to 32K)	4 or 5 of 30 to 60 minutes	1 or 2 off or easy "cross"
8	5K to 10K race or fast training	4 or 5 of 30 to 60 minutes	1 or 2 off or easy "cross"
9	9 to 10 miles (15 to 16K)	4 or 5 of 30 to 60 minutes	1 or 2 off or easy "cross"
10	20 to 22 miles (32 to 35K)	4 or 5 of 30 to 60 minutes	1 or 2 off or easy "cross"
11	5K to 10K race or 10 to 11 miles (16 to 18K)	4 or 5 of 30 to 60 minutes	1 or 2 off or easy "cross"
12	1 hour	4 or 5 of 30 to 60 minutes	1 or 2 off or easy "cross"
13	None	4 or 5 of about 30 minutes	2 or 3 off or easy "cross"
14	Marathon race	None	1 off
15	None	3 or 4 short and easy	3 or 4 off or easy "cross"

The writing on the left-hand page for each day is mine. But the most important part of the book is what *you* write on the right-hand page. This is the diary page for each day.

I suggest a schedule at the beginning of each week, which you're free to modify. Tailor it to your needs, then list the exact training you plan to do on each of the seven days that follow. Later add the details as you complete the scheduled session. Fill in the blanks, and check and circle the options that apply to you as you write yourself a great success story for this marathon a day at a time.

A sample log page follows. You can photocopy this page to use in your program if you're using this book to train for another marathon after filling these 100 pages.

RACERS

Week	Long day	Fast day	Other runs	Rest days
1	12 to 14 miles (20 to 22K)	1 to 3 miles (1.6 to 5K)	4 of 30 to 60 minutes	1 off or "cross"
2	14 to 16 miles (22 to 25K)	1 to 3 miles (1.6 to 5K)	4 of 30 to 60 minutes	1 off or "cross"
3	7 to 8 miles (11 to 13K)	5K to 10K race	4 of 30 to 60 minutes	1 off or "cross"
4	16 to 18 miles (26 to 29K)	1 to 3 miles (1.6 to 5K)	4 of 30 to 60 minutes	1 off or "cross"
5	18 to 20 miles (29 to 32K)	1 to 3 miles (1.6 to 5K)	4 of 30 to 60 minutes	1 off or "cross"
6	9 to 10 miles (14 to 16K)	5K to 10K race	4 of 30 to 60 minutes	1 off or "cross"
7	20 to 22 miles (32 to 35K)	1 to 3 miles (1.6 to 5K)	4 of 30 to 60 minutes	1 off or "cross"
8	21 to 23 miles (33 to 37K)	1 to 3 miles (1.6 to 5K)	4 of 30 to 60 minutes	1 off or "cross"
9	10 to 11 miles (16 to 18K)	5K to 10K race	4 of 30 to 60 minutes	1 off or "cross"
10	22 to 24 miles (35 to 38K)	1 to 3 miles (1.6 to 5K)	4 of 30 to 60 minutes	1 off or "cross"
11	11 to 12 miles (18 to 19K)	5K to 10K race	4 of 30 to 60 minutes	1 off or "cross"
12	1 hour	1 to 3 miles (1.6 to 5K)	4 of 30 to 60 minutes	1 off or "cross"
13	None	None	4 to 6 of about 30 minutes	1 to 3 off or "cross"
14	Marathon race	None	None	1 off
15	None	None	3 or 4 short and easy	3 or 4 off or "cross"

Date _____ **Plans** _____

Training Session

Type of run   □ long   □ fast   □ easy   □ none   □ race

Distance _____ **Time** _____

Pace _____ per mile   _____ per kilometer

Splits _____ / _____ / _____ / _____ / _____ / _____

Effort   □ max   □ hard   □ moderate   □ easy   □ rest

Training heart rates   target _____   actual _____

Warm-up _____ **Cool-down** _____ **Cross-training** _____

Training Conditions

Location _____ **Time of day** _____

People   □ alone   □ with group   □ race   □ with partner _____
                                                                             name

Surface   □ road   □ trail   □ track   □ mixed _____

Terrain   □ flat   □ hilly   □ mixed _____

Weather _____ **Shoes worn** _____

Diet   drinks during run _____   foods during run _____

Training Rating

Success level   10   9   8   7   6   5   4   3   2   1   0

Training Comments

_____

_____

_____

Marathon raceday is your graduation day. You earn these final hours on the big stage with dozens of days spent training.

STARTING NOW

Your marathon starts now, this week, three months before the event itself. Whatever your starting point or your goal is, you schedule the first long run of the training cycle this week. It probably is longer than you've run in quite a while—or perhaps ever—so hold down the pace. Remember how much farther you still have to go. Choose your program from the options listed, assign runs to the next seven days of diary pages, and add details there for completed training.

Cruiser Program

Big day: Long run of 12 to 14 miles (20 to 22K) with a mix of running and walking (run no more than 1 mile—1.6K—at a time, and walk for at least one minute). Run-walk this distance no faster than your projected marathon pace.

Other training days: Three or four easy runs of 30 to 45 minutes each, with walking breaks optional.

Rest days: Two or three with no running, but possibly easy cross-training.

Pacer Program

Big day: Long run of 12 to 14 miles (20 to 22K) with walking breaks optional (if used, run at least 1 mile—1.6K—and walk no more than one minute). Run this distance about one minute per mile slower (35 seconds per kilometer) than your projected marathon pace.

Other training days: Four to five easy runs of 30 to 60 minutes each.

Rest days: One or two with no running, but possibly easy cross-training.

Racer Program

Long day: 12 to 14 miles (20 to 22K). Run about one minute per mile (35 seconds per kilometer) slower than your projected marathon pace.

Fast day: 1- to 3-mile (1.6 to 5K) run at current 10K race pace. (This may be broken into shorter intervals that total 1 to 3 miles—1.6 to 5K—not counting recovery periods.) Warm up and cool down with easy running.

Other training days: Four easy runs of 30 to 60 minutes each.

Rest days: One with no running, but possibly easy cross-training.

30-Month Marathon

Marathons don't start at the starting line. They are almost finished when you get this far into the full marathon experience.

What you will do now is largely ordained by what you did in the months that brought you here. Some runners even call the race itself a "victory lap." It was that for me when I lined up in May 1998 at the Vancouver International Marathon. This event was 30 months in the making for me, and nothing that happened in the next few hours could dull the celebration.

The drought began 2-1/2 years earlier, when a case of persistent dizziness settled into my head during the recovery period from the recent Royal Victoria Marathon. This malady was scary at first, when doctors mentioned the worst possibilities (heart disease and brain tumor) but then ruled them out. The struggle to maintain physical stability remained for a while, and finally the minor spells of wooziness became no more than a nuisance.

By then I'd fallen out of two-marathons-a-year rhythm of the early 1990s. I never said "never again" but did wonder when I'd start running this far again.

I had several false starts in the previous two years. Illnesses stopped the Sacramento 1996 and San Diego 1997 marathons short of their starting lines, and work conflicts did the same to Boston and Sacramento in 1997.

TRAINING TIP

View the marathon as the Mount Everest of running. It's a peak that every runner dreams of scaling at least once. You too can stand at the top, but not without a long and well-planned climb.

Reasons not to try a marathon are easy to find. That's why every Average Joe doesn't run one. This Joe wanted to become less average again.

Date _____ **Plans** _____

Training Session

Type of run   ☐ long   ☐ fast   ☐ easy   ☐ none   ☐ race

Distance _____   **Time** _____

Pace _____ per mile   _____ per kilometer

Splits _____ / _____ / _____ / _____ / _____ / _____

Effort   ☐ max   ☐ hard   ☐ moderate   ☐ easy   ☐ rest

Training heart rates   target _____   actual _____

Warm-up _____   **Cool-down** _____   **Cross-training** _____

Training Conditions

Location _____   **Time of day** _____

People   ☐ alone   ☐ with group   ☐ race   ☐ with partner _____
                                                                name

Surface   ☐ road   ☐ trail   ☐ track   ☐ mixed _____

Terrain   ☐ flat   ☐ hilly   ☐ mixed _____

Weather _____   **Shoes worn** _____

Diet   drinks during run _____   foods during run _____

Training Rating

Success level   10   9   8   7   6   5   4   3   2   1   0

Training Comments

_____

_____

_____

Victory Lap

A ready excuse surfaced for skipping the 1998 Vancouver International Marathon. I shuffled sore-footed through the long training runs, which still fell well short of marathon length.

Then Amby Burfoot told me, with his actions and not his words, to quit babying myself. The *Runner's World* editor was a self-confessed "mess" before his recent Boston Marathon and still got to the starting line.

Not starting is like dropping out during a race. Doing either one is habit forming, and it was time for me to break this habit at Vancouver. Why here? Because the race officials had treated me kindly with five straight years of invitations, but mostly because Vancouver was only about 42K from where my marathoning had left off in Victoria 2-1/2 years earlier.

I lined up beside Diane Palmason, who aimed this day to break the world record for women over 60. (She would miss by less than a minute with 3:16.) Diane asked, "What do you hope to do today?" I simply said, "Finish." But a more honest answer would have been that I'd already met my goal by coming this far.

The hardest part of a marathon is getting to its starting line. I was finally there. Once you get to the start, you're almost guaranteed to reach the other end. And I did.

TRAINING TIP

Realize that your marathon finish line is nearer than you imagine. If you can race as little as 10K, you can tack on the remaining 20 miles with a few more months of training.

My finish wasn't pretty, and the time isn't worth a public mention. But this was a victory lap at every step, a celebration of being back in this game after spending too long on the bench.

Date _____ **Plans** _____

Training Session

Type of run   ☐ long   ☐ fast   ☐ easy   ☐ none   ☐ race

Distance _____ **Time** _____

Pace _____ per mile   _____ per kilometer

Splits _____ / _____ / _____ / _____ / _____ / _____

Effort   ☐ max   ☐ hard   ☐ moderate   ☐ easy   ☐ rest

Training heart rates target _____ actual _____

Warm-up _____ **Cool-down** _____ **Cross-training** _____

Training Conditions

Location _____ **Time of day** _____

People ☐ alone   ☐ with group   ☐ race   ☐ with partner _____
name

Surface   ☐ road   ☐ trail   ☐ track   ☐ mixed _____

Terrain   ☐ flat   ☐ hilly   ☐ mixed _____

Weather _____ **Shoes worn** _____

Diet   drinks during run _____   foods during run _____

Training Rating

Success level   10   9   8   7   6   5   4   3   2   1   0

Training Comments

_____

_____

_____

Messages to Marathoners

Such is the state of the sport today that you likely are either a marathoner or have one close to you. You or your surrogate probably are training for or recovering from a marathon right now. I wasn't as this book passed through editing. But I remain part of the marathon family by encouraging and advising individual marathoners almost daily and by speaking to them in groups and watching them race monthly.

My message to marathoners is more motivational than informational. The pep talk takes one or more of these paths:

- You're lucky to be here now. Never have so many of you with such widely ranging abilities been made to feel so welcome. Never have runners enjoyed so much valuable technical support and the more important emotional support. Now is the best time to be a marathoner.

- I know you. Maybe your names and faces are unfamiliar. But I know you by the training you're doing, by how you will feel on race day, and by the memories that you carry. I haven't done any of this for a while, but these are experiences you don't forget. Our sharing of them brings us into the same community of marathoners.

- I admire you. I don't come to you as an expert imparting wisdom. Instead I bow in respect for what you are doing. You inspire me. I hope that what you're doing now can have the same effect on others who watch you do it. Marathoning can be contagious.

TRAINING TIP

Don't think you must turn over your whole life to training. Your long run will become much longer than it has been. But you'll run normally—or even slightly *easier* than usual—the other days.

Date _____ **Plans** _____

Training Session

Type of run   □ long   □ fast   □ easy   □ none   □ race

Distance _____ **Time** _____

Pace _____ per mile   _____ per kilometer

Splits _____ / _____ / _____ / _____ / _____ / _____

Effort   □ max   □ hard   □ moderate   □ easy   □ rest

Training heart rates target _____ actual _____

Warm-up _____ **Cool-down** _____ **Cross-training** _____

Training Conditions

Location _____ **Time of day** _____

People □ alone   □ with group   □ race   □ with partner _____
name

Surface   □ road   □ trail   □ track   □ mixed _____

Terrain   □ flat   □ hilly   □ mixed _____

Weather _____ **Shoes worn** _____

Diet   drinks during run _____   foods during run _____

Training Rating

Success level   10   9   8   7   6   5   4   3   2   1   0

Training Comments

_____

_____

_____

_____

More Messages

Adding to the list started on day 3:

- You can't fake a marathon. Maybe you can wake up one morning and decide to run a 5K or 10K that same day. But few of us normally run far enough to jump into a marathon without special training. The long-term demands of marathons enhance their attraction and prolong the memories.

- The marathon is brutally and beautifully honest. You get back on race day almost exactly what you invested earlier. There's only one way you can buy a decent marathon—not with your cash or credit cards, not with your fame or power, but only with proper preparation. If you don't pay in advance with training, you pay later in pain.

- The marathon can humble you. No truer line has ever been written than that one by Bill Rodgers. He has broken 2:10 but also has broken down and dropped out (which means four-, five-, and six-hour marathoners who finished that day can say they "beat" Rodgers). Even with the best of training, you're still not home free until the marathon ends as well as you hoped it would—or better.

- The marathon can make you proud. If the distance can humble the proudest of us, then the reverse is equally true. It can make proud the humblest of us. I'm bothered by marathoners who say, "I'm only a back-of-the-packer," or, "I'm only a run-walker." No apologies accepted. Take pride in your marathon, however long your race might last.

TRAINING TIP

Schedule the three elements common to all effective programs: long runs, fast runs, and easy days. Only the amount of each ingredient and the pace of each run differ from runner to runner and from program to program.

Date _____ **Plans** _____

Training Session

Type of run ☐ long ☐ fast ☐ easy ☐ none ☐ race

Distance _____ **Time** _____

Pace _____ per mile _____ per kilometer

Splits _____ / _____ / _____ / _____ / _____ / _____

Effort ☐ max ☐ hard ☐ moderate ☐ easy ☐ rest

Training heart rates target _____ actual _____

Warm-up _____ **Cool-down** _____ **Cross-training** _____

Training Conditions

Location _____ **Time of day** _____

People ☐ alone ☐ with group ☐ race ☐ with partner _____
name

Surface ☐ road ☐ trail ☐ track ☐ mixed _____

Terrain ☐ flat ☐ hilly ☐ mixed _____

Weather _____ **Shoes worn** _____

Diet drinks during run _____ foods during run _____

Training Rating

Success level 10 9 8 7 6 5 4 3 2 1 0

Training Comments

_____

_____

_____

One in a Thousand

This year alone the total finishes in U.S. marathons will number nearly a half-million. Note the word is *finishes*. The number of *finishers*—individual American runners who complete marathons, counting them once even though they run the distance multiple times—is smaller but still huge. You might think this figure shrinks your effort to insignificance. It's hard to brag that your finish time ranks you 202,000th for the year.

But let's find you some glory in those numbers. If you really want to know where you stand, don't count how many runners finish ahead of you. Instead, turn around and look behind you. Look especially at the people you can't see: those who trained for a marathon but didn't reach the starting line . . . who race but not at this distance . . . who run but never race . . . who used to run but don't anymore . . . who never ran and never will.

TRAINING TIP

Plan to train far enough to cope with the race distance. This, of course, is your most important concern in preparing for the marathon, because almost no one can run nearly this far without greatly increasing training mileage.

Which brings us back to that figure of a half-million marathon finishes a year. Eliminate the multiple finishes of some runners, subtract visitors from other countries, and the true count of American marathoners is still huge. It stands at about a quarter-million—this from a national population of a quarter-billion.

Being a marathoner makes you one in a thousand Americans. Pat yourself on the back for doing something that 99.9 percent of your countrymen or women couldn't or wouldn't do.

Don't call yourself slow, because you are not. You are fast enough to beat everyone who isn't in the race.

Date _____ *Plans* _____

Training Session

Type of run □ long □ fast □ easy □ none □ race

Distance _____ *Time* _____

Pace _____ per mile _____ per kilometer

Splits _____ / _____ / _____ / _____ / _____ / _____

Effort □ max □ hard □ moderate □ easy □ rest

Training heart rates target _____ actual _____

Warm-up _____ *Cool-down* _____ *Cross-training* _____

Training Conditions

Location _____ *Time of day* _____

People □ alone □ with group □ race □ with partner _____
                                                             name

Surface □ road □ trail □ track □ mixed _____

Terrain □ flat □ hilly □ mixed _____

Weather _____ *Shoes worn* _____

Diet drinks during run _____ foods during run _____

Training Rating

Success level 10 9 8 7 6 5 4 3 2 1 0

Training Comments

_____

_____

_____

Max Effort

Footnotes, the official magazine of the Road Runners Club of America, carried several opinions on who is or isn't a true marathoner. One letter, typical of the group, read, "I think [marathons] should turn off the clock after five hours and consider the race over. If you cannot finish under five hours, you have no business running a marathon."

My answer isn't a true rebuttal but a story. When I started teaching running classes at the University of Oregon, a student showed up carrying a motorcycle helmet and wearing a tough expression. The look seemed to say, "Prove to me that you're any good as a teacher. If not, I'm out of here." I didn't yet know that the look really said, "Do I belong here?" The roster listed her name as Angela Skorodinsky, a grad student who was 32 at the time. But when I asked what she preferred to be called, she wrote "Max." It fit—short and strong, just like her.

The class began with a timed mile. Not an all-out mile race but a simple run to draw a fitness baseline. Max lagged a half-lap behind anyone else, running (with some walking) 11-1/2 minutes. Afterward she complained about how hard it had been, how finishing so far back had embarrassed her, how she might look for a different fitness class.

TRAINING TIP

Plan to train fast enough to handle the marathon's pace (if you are a Pacer concerned with time or a Racer who wants to place well). Pace training includes semilong runs at marathon tempo or slightly faster.

I wouldn't let Max leave. Neither of us could have guessed then that two years later Max could proudly call herself a true marathoner.

She showed me what I'd long known but seldom seen so closely. There's almost no end to the distance someone can run with persistence.

Date _____ **Plans** _____

Training Session

Type of run ☐ long ☐ fast ☐ easy ☐ none ☐ race

Distance _____ **Time** _____

Pace _____ per mile _____ per kilometer

Splits _____ / _____ / _____ / _____ / _____ / _____

Effort ☐ max ☐ hard ☐ moderate ☐ easy ☐ rest

Training heart rates target _____ actual _____

Warm-up _____ **Cool-down** _____ **Cross-training** _____

Training Conditions

Location _____ **Time of day** _____

People ☐ alone ☐ with group ☐ race ☐ with partner _____
                                                                    name

Surface ☐ road ☐ trail ☐ track ☐ mixed _____

Terrain ☐ flat ☐ hilly ☐ mixed _____

Weather _____ **Shoes worn** _____

Diet drinks during run _____ foods during run _____

Training Rating

Success level   10   9   8   7   6   5   4   3   2   1   0

Training Comments

_____

_____

_____

A True Marathoner

My student, Max Skorodinsky, decided without any prodding from her teacher that she would run the Portland Marathon. She wrote her own training plan.

I only saw her a few times all summer, but she e-mailed me regularly with progress reports. She listed a pair of two-hour-plus runs.

Her "midterm test" of marathon training was a local half-marathon race. There she averaged the same 11-plus mile pace that she could only carry for a single mile on her first day of class. "Damn, that's a long way!" she said at the finish line. "Now I have to think about going twice this far." I assured her she'd be okay if she did the needed training between July and October. She did it.

The 2002 Portland Marathon was a first for me: the first time I'd ever watched students finish a marathon that had started for them in my classes. I felt more nervous for them than I've ever felt for myself at marathons. I greeted them with more tears than I've shed at all my marathons combined.

TRAINING TIP

Counterbalance the long and fast sessions with easy days. More races are lost by training too long, too fast, or too often than by running too short, too slow, or too seldom.

The last of the students to arrive was Max. I figured she would take about 5-1/2 hours. She ran 5:08, averaging the mile pace from her first day in running class for 26 times the original distance.

Max puts a human face on the five-hour marathoner. Would anyone who says that this is too slow to count dare to look her in the eyes and say she doesn't belong?

A five-hour marathon isn't slow. Slow is starting a race and not finishing, stopping training before the race starts, or never starting to train.

Date _____ *Plans* _____

Training Session

Type of run ☐ long ☐ fast ☐ easy ☐ none ☐ race

Distance _____ *Time* _____

Pace _____ per mile _____ per kilometer

Splits _____ / _____ / _____ / _____ / _____ / _____

Effort ☐ max ☐ hard ☐ moderate ☐ easy ☐ rest

Training heart rates target _____ actual _____

Warm-up _____ *Cool-down* _____ *Cross-training* _____

Training Conditions

Location _____ *Time of day* _____

People ☐ alone ☐ with group ☐ race ☐ with partner _____
name

Surface ☐ road ☐ trail ☐ track ☐ mixed _____

Terrain ☐ flat ☐ hilly ☐ mixed _____

Weather _____ *Shoes worn* _____

Diet drinks during run _____ foods during run _____

Training Rating

Success level 10 9 8 7 6 5 4 3 2 1 0

Training Comments

_____

_____

_____

Marathon training is long and tough, as is the race. But you can't run hard and fast every day without risking a breakdown.

STAYING WELL

Note that one to three days off each week are scheduled for rest, and several others are easy. The number of rest days and type of easy days remain the same throughout your program. They become more important than ever as the hard runs grow harder. Rest and easy days allow the hard work to work. They protect you from running yourself into exhaustion and injury. Choose your program from the options listed, assign runs to the next seven days of diary pages, and add details there for completed training.

Cruiser Program

Big day: Semilong run of 6 to 7 miles (10 to 11K), or half the distance of last week's long one. Run this distance nonstop with no walking breaks. Run slightly faster than your projected marathon pace.

Other training days: Three or four easy runs of 30 to 45 minutes each, with walking breaks optional.

Rest days: Two or three with no running, but possibly easy cross-training.

Pacer Program

Big day: Semilong run of 6 to 7 miles (10 to 11K), or half the distance of last week's long one. Run this distance nonstop at your projected marathon pace or slightly faster.

Other training days: Four or five easy runs of 30 to 60 minutes each.

Rest days: One or two with no running, but possibly easy cross-training.

Racer Program

Long day: 14 to 16 miles (22 to 25K), or about a 2-mile (3K) increase from your last one. Run about one minute per mile (35 seconds per kilometer) slower than your projected marathon pace.

Fast day: 1- to 3-mile (1.5 to 5K) run at current 10K race pace. (This may be broken into shorter intervals that total 1 to 3 miles—1.5 to 5K—not counting recovery periods.) Warm up and cool down with easy running.

Other training days: Four easy runs of 30 to 60 minutes each.

Rest days: One with no running, but possibly easy cross-training.

Trial Mile

The mile holds a special place in my memory. This was the first distance I ever ran for time, almost a half-century ago. I've raced the mile more often than all other distances combined.

But my best mile isn't one that netted me a state high school title. It isn't one of several that ended before 4-1/2 minutes had ticked away. These times are pleasant but ancient memories.

My best mile is as fresh as today's run. It takes twice as long to complete as those old races and is my slowest mile of any day. But it's the best mile because it gets me going and sometimes makes me stop.

I read about Kenyan Cosmas Ndeti before one of his Boston Marathon victories. The line that influenced me most: "He has been known to wake up, run for a kilometer, then climb back into bed."

TRAINING TIP

Never forget that racing—especially at marathon length—is uncomfortable. You can't improve without sometimes venturing into discomfort. But these occasional ventures must be separated by returns to your comfort zone.

When this story appeared, I was limping through a spell of Achilles tendinitis. It had lingered for more than a month as I'd tried to tough out "easy" half-hour runs.

Taking a clue from Ndeti, I listened more closely to what the Achilles tendon told me each morning. Because "miles" and not "meters" is my first language, I ran a mile and then decided what to do next. If signs of trouble appeared or didn't clear, and especially if they worsened, I forced myself to stop for that day and try again the next. The pain eased within a few days and disappeared within two weeks.

Date _____ Plans _____

Training Session

Type of run ☐ long ☐ fast ☐ easy ☐ none ☐ race

Distance _____ **Time** _____

Pace _____ per mile _____ per kilometer

Splits _____ / _____ / _____ / _____ / _____ / _____

Effort ☐ max ☐ hard ☐ moderate ☐ easy ☐ rest

Training heart rates target _____ actual _____

Warm-up _____ **Cool-down** _____ **Cross-training** _____

Training Conditions

Location _____ **Time of day** _____

People ☐ alone ☐ with group ☐ race ☐ with partner _____
name

Surface ☐ road ☐ trail ☐ track ☐ mixed _____

Terrain ☐ flat ☐ hilly ☐ mixed _____

Weather _____ **Shoes worn** _____

Diet drinks during run _____ foods during run _____

Training Rating

Success level 10 9 8 7 6 5 4 3 2 1 0

Training Comments

_____

_____

_____

Time of Truth

You might ask, Why even bother running a trial mile? Why not just decide whether to run before dressing and going out the door?

"Listen to your body," we're told, and let it be the judge of what to do or not do. But what do we listen for, and when? The truth is that the body lies before most runs. We need a better test of feelings than what it says at rest.

If I heeded all signals of stiffness, soreness, and simple resting inertia before the start, I would skip half my runs. And I'd go too far or fast in the other half when enthusiasm overrode the warning signals.

Right before the run is the wrong time to listen to the body. That's when it likes to tell its biggest fibs—trying to convince you that it feels better or worse than it really does.

TRAINING TIP

Don't swallow the most damaging myth in athletics: "Pain equals gain." No one can stand to train painfully all the time. All you gain from that suffering is ever-increasing pain—until you can't or won't tolerate it any longer.

Sometimes running injuries go into hibernation between runs. You tell yourself at the start that you're okay, you try to run as planned, you overdo, the pain comes out of hiding, and you suffer a setback by not stopping soon enough. Just as often, though, the problem feels worst when you're not running. You think before starting that you're hurting and need another day off, when warm-up might have worked out the stiffness and soreness.

The trial mile acts as a truth serum. It gets you out the door and then 10 minutes later tells you honestly what you can do that day. Listen. Run as you feel, yes, but as you're feeling after the warm-up and not before it started.

Date _____ **Plans** _____

Training Session

Type of run □ long □ fast □ easy □ none □ race

Distance _____ **Time** _____

Pace _____ per mile _____ per kilometer

Splits _____ / _____ / _____ / _____ / _____ / _____

Effort □ max □ hard □ moderate □ easy □ rest

Training heart rates target _____ actual _____

Warm-up _____ **Cool-down** _____ **Cross-training** _____

Training Conditions

Location _____ **Time of day** _____

People □ alone □ with group □ race □ with partner _____

name

Surface □ road □ trail □ track □ mixed _____

Terrain □ flat □ hilly □ mixed _____

Weather _____ **Shoes worn** _____

Diet drinks during run _____ foods during run _____

Training Rating

Success level   10   9   8   7   6   5   4   3   2   1   0

Training Comments

_____

_____

_____

Do-It-Yourself Doctoring

I'm not a doctor, but I often play one in my working life. Questions about running medicine come my way almost every day. I decline to guess at specific diagnoses and plead ignorance to medical treatments, despite having soaked up a little medical knowledge from editing the books of four different doctors. But I do talk in general terms about getting hurt and getting well. In that area I am an expert, having plenty of practice at recovering.

TRAINING TIP

Think of the marathon as an unnatural act. Exciting and challenging as this race (as well as the training that mimics it) might be, it tears you down, and you must build back up after each hard effort with many easier ones.

Most running injuries are self-inflicted. So if you've hurt yourself, you can also make yourself better again. That is to say, your health is mostly your own responsibility and not a doctor's.

Fortunately, few running ailments are permanent. Nearly all of them heal, and fairly quickly, with simple self-help steps that are remarkably similar no matter where the specific problem is—hip to toe and anywhere in between. This I can tell you about suffering and rehabilitating injuries:

- They are likely, if not inevitable. Almost everyone who runs gets hurt eventually, and almost everyone gets better soon.

- They are minor. Seldom do these injuries interfere with normal life, or require a doctor's help, or involve extensive and expensive care.

- They are self-inflicted. Usually they result not from "accidents" but from the Big Four mistakes—running too far, too fast, too soon, too often.

- They are treatable. Usually they respond quickly to simple adjustments in training type and amount.

- They allow activity. If it isn't reduced running, then it can be an agreeable alternative.

Date _____ *Plans* _____

Training Session

Type of run   ☐ long   ☐ fast   ☐ easy   ☐ none   ☐ race

Distance _____ *Time* _____

Pace _____ per mile   _____ per kilometer

Splits _____ / _____ / _____ / _____ / _____ / _____

Effort   ☐ max   ☐ hard   ☐ moderate   ☐ easy   ☐ rest

Training heart rates target _____ actual _____

Warm-up _____ *Cool-down* _____ *Cross-training* _____

Training Conditions

Location _____ *Time of day* _____

People ☐ alone ☐ with group ☐ race ☐ with partner _____
                                                                        name

Surface   ☐ road   ☐ trail   ☐ track   ☐ mixed _____

Terrain   ☐ flat   ☐ hilly   ☐ mixed _____

Weather _____ *Shoes worn* _____

Diet   drinks during run _____   foods during run _____

Training Rating

Success level   10   9   8   7   6   5   4   3   2   1   0

Training Comments

_____

_____

_____

Your Friend Pain

A young friend of mine, a student named Amanda from one of my running classes at the University of Oregon, jumped up her mileage too quickly. The result was predictable and more painful than usual in such cases. She suffered a suspected stress fracture in her upper leg.

The doctor said Amanda would need a bone scan to confirm these suspicions. "How much will that cost?" she asked. When she heard an amount that would cut too deeply into her student budget, she said, "And if it is a stress fracture, what will the treatment be?" No cast and no medicine, she was told; just no running for at least six weeks.

Amanda decided she didn't need a definitive diagnosis. She already wasn't running but was substituting water running while the leg recovered. She was practicing a do-it-herself doctoring plan that many runners need to employ occasionally.

TRAINING TIP

Alternate hard and easy days only if you are an elite athlete. Most runners are slow to rebound from hard days, and one big session each *week* is about all the midpack finisher can tolerate.

Let's say an injury has knocked you off your feet. A doctor can only diagnose why you're hurting and suggest what to do about it. *You* are responsible for your rehab.

Your best friend when you're injured isn't a medical professional; it's your own pain. It tells you what you can and can't do while recovering.

Whatever the specifics of what ails you, there is a path back to health that lets you heal and still stay active, fit, and sane. Choose an activity type and level that let you keep moving without aggravating the problem that has limited or stopped your running.

Your choice isn't between running or nothing. It's between what hurts and what doesn't.

Date _____ **Plans** _____

Training Session

Type of run   □ long   □ fast   □ easy   □ none   □ race

Distance _____   **Time** _____

Pace _____ per mile   _____ per kilometer

Splits _____ / _____ / _____ / _____ / _____ / _____

Effort   □ max   □ hard   □ moderate   □ easy   □ rest

Training heart rates target _____   actual _____

Warm-up _____   **Cool-down** _____   **Cross-training** _____

Training Conditions

Location _____   **Time of day** _____

People □ alone   □ with group   □ race   □ with partner _____
name

Surface   □ road   □ trail   □ track   □ mixed _____

Terrain   □ flat   □ hilly   □ mixed _____

Weather _____   **Shoes worn** _____

Diet   drinks during run _____   foods during run _____

Training Rating

Success level   10   9   8   7   6   5   4   3   2   1   0

Training Comments

_____

_____

_____

Steps to Health

If injured, work back through these stages of rehab:

1. If walking is painful and running is impossible, bike or swim for the usual running time periods. These activities take nearly all pressure off most injuries while still allowing steady effort.

2. If walking is relatively pain-free but running still hurts, start to walk as soon as you can move ahead without limping or increasing the pain. Observe these warnings—no limping, no increasing pain—at all stages of recovery.

3. If walking is easy and some running is possible, add intervals of slow running—as little as one minute in five at first, then gradually building up the amount of running until you reach the next stage.

4. If running pain eases but minor discomfort persists, the balance tips in favor of running mixed with walking. Insert brief walks at this stage when you can't yet tolerate steady pressure. Many injuries respond better to intermittent running than to the steady type.

5. If all pain and tenderness are blessedly gone, run steadily again. But approach it cautiously for a while as you regain lost fitness. Run a little more slowly than normal, with no long or fast efforts until you can handle the short-slow runs comfortably.

It's good to repeat yourself at this stage. Run laps instead of a single big loop to give yourself a place to stop a run early without being miles from home.

A patient patient knows when to stop. Cutting short a run during rehab isn't a sign of weakness but of wisdom.

TRAINING TIP

Recover actively, if you wish. Recovery doesn't require complete rest (although at least one day off a week is highly recommended). You can recover while still satisfying the urge to run by running easily.

Date _____ *Plans* _____

Training Session

Type of run   □ long   □ fast   □ easy   □ none   □ race

Distance _____   *Time* _____

Pace _____ per mile   _____ per kilometer

Splits _____ / _____ / _____ / _____ / _____ / _____

Effort   □ max   □ hard   □ moderate   □ easy   □ rest

Training heart rates target _____ actual _____

Warm-up _____ *Cool-down* _____ *Cross-training* _____

Training Conditions

Location _____ *Time of day* _____

People   □ alone   □ with group   □ race   □ with partner _____
                                                                                                   name

Surface   □ road   □ trail   □ track   □ mixed _____

Terrain   □ flat   □ hilly   □ mixed _____

Weather _____   *Shoes worn* _____

Diet   drinks during run _____   foods during run _____

Training Rating

Success level   10   9   8   7   6   5   4   3   2   1   0

Training Comments

_____

_____

_____

Stretching a Point

I came into running at a time when the only stretches that distance runners did were the backstretch and homestretch of a track. Stretching of the standing-still variety? I never did any; I never thought a runner needed any. This all changed in the 1970s for me and for the sport. A doctor treating a stubborn injury asked me to bend over and touch my toes. I strained to graze my shins just below the knees. I've stretched ever since, with varying degrees of commitment and success.

Thirty years later, the practice of stretching had its worth questioned. A study in a British medical journal stated that stretching does little if any good in preventing injury, easing soreness, or improving performance. Those were the very reasons we'd stretched all this time.

Runners asked me whether they should stop stretching or said they were right all along not to stretch. I noted that the practice would have faded away long ago if it had been identified as worthless or harmful, yet it has remained a mainstay of training.

TRAINING TIP

Stay well within the comfort zone on easy days. For experienced runners this might mean comfortably paced runs of up to an hour. Newer marathoners shouldn't feel guilty about doing as little as a half-hour.

Runners won't suddenly stop stretching now, any more than we'd stop running on hearing one negative report of its effects. But the questioning of stretching does lead us to take a close look at how and when we stretch and what it might and might not do for us.

I still stretch, regularly if minimally. Each run ends with a few minutes of bending and reaching because I perceive benefits that are subtle but real.

Date _____ *Plans* _____

Training Session

Type of run □ long   □ fast   □ easy   □ none   □ race

Distance _____   *Time* _____

Pace _____ per mile   _____ per kilometer

Splits _____ / _____ / _____ / _____ / _____ / _____

Effort □ max   □ hard   □ moderate   □ easy   □ rest

Training heart rates target _____   actual _____

Warm-up _____ *Cool-down* _____ *Cross-training* _____

Training Conditions

Location _____ *Time of day* _____

People □ alone   □ with group   □ race   □ with partner _____
                                                                            name

Surface □ road   □ trail   □ track   □ mixed _____

Terrain □ flat   □ hilly   □ mixed _____

Weather _____ *Shoes worn* _____

Diet drinks during run _____   foods during run _____

Training Rating

Success level   10   9   8   7   6   5   4   3   2   1   0

Training Comments

_____

_____

_____

_____

Why Stretch?

Stretching is neither a panacea nor a pain. The bad press it has received hasn't changed my practice of it or my views on the subject, which are as follows:

1. Stretching is an overrated requirement. Runners become tight-muscled as a normal and necessary adaptation to the activity. Otherwise why would running do this to us? A certain degree of inflexibility is to be expected and accepted, but "tight enough" can lead to "too tight" without some corrective action.

2. Stretching isn't just for running. What's good for running might not be right for overall fitness. Anyone seeking balanced fitness needs to counteract the supertightening of running with some exercise that gives the opposite result.

3. Stretching doesn't eliminate injuries. Done wrong—too aggressively and too much—stretches cause more problems than they prevent. Done right—gently and in small doses—stretches still don't override the effects of running unwisely.

4. Stretching isn't a warm-up. It doesn't start you sweating or raise your heart rate. You warm up by moving—first by running slowly or walking, then by easing into the full pace of the day.

5. Stretching is a cool-down. Warm muscles respond best to these exercises. Run first, then stretch. This also gives you a few extra minutes to cool down before you sit down.

6. Stretching is a sign of maturity. The youthful, new runner is naturally more flexible than the older, long-time one. Put another way, the more years you have in life and in running, the more that stretching might help you.

TRAINING TIP

Treat the easy runs as the meat and potatoes (or beans and rice, if you're vegetarian) of the running diet. The dessert comes in small, infrequent portions of racing and training and abnormal distances and speeds.

Date _____ **Plans** _____

Training Session

Type of run   ☐ long   ☐ fast   ☐ easy   ☐ none   ☐ race

Distance _____ **Time** _____

Pace _____ per mile _____ per kilometer

Splits _____ / _____ / _____ / _____ / _____ / _____

Effort   ☐ max   ☐ hard   ☐ moderate   ☐ easy   ☐ rest

Training heart rates   target _____   actual _____

Warm-up _____ **Cool-down** _____ **Cross-training** _____

Training Conditions

Location _____ **Time of day** _____

People   ☐ alone   ☐ with group   ☐ race   ☐ with partner _____
                                                                    name

Surface   ☐ road   ☐ trail   ☐ track   ☐ mixed _____

Terrain   ☐ flat   ☐ hilly   ☐ mixed _____

Weather _____ **Shoes worn** _____

Diet   drinks during run _____   foods during run _____

Training Rating

Success level   10   9   8   7   6   5   4   3   2   1   0

Training Comments

_____

_____

_____

The long run is the centerpiece of your marathon training program. Step up its distance slowly and recover well afterward.

GOING LONG

This week's training tips deal entirely with running long. So let's take a few moments to consider the flip side of longer running, which is not running at all. On nonrun days, you don't need total rest but only a break from the pounding of running. You can cross-train on some or all of those days—with biking, swimming, running in water, and walking being your best alternatives. Choose your program from the options listed, assign runs to the next seven days of diary pages, and add details there for completed training.

Cruiser Program

Big day: Race of 5K, or fast solo run of 1 to 3 miles (1.6 to 5K). In all cases, run at least one minute per mile (35 seconds per kilometer) faster than your projected marathon pace.

Other training days: Three or four easy runs of 30 to 45 minutes each, with walking breaks optional.

Rest days: Two or three with no running, but possibly easy cross-training.

Pacer Program

Big day: Long run of 14 to 16 miles (22 to 25K), or about a 2-mile (3K) increase from your last one. Walking breaks are optional. Run about one minute per mile (35 seconds per kilometer) slower than your projected marathon pace.

Other training days: Four or five easy runs of 30 to 60 minutes each.

Rest days: One or two with no running, but possibly easy cross-training.

Racer Program

Long day: Semilong run of 7 to 8 miles (11 to 13K), or half the distance of last week's long one. Run at your projected marathon pace or slightly faster.

Fast day: Race of 5K to 10K, or 1- to 3-mile (1.6 to 5K) run at current 10K race pace. (This may be broken into shorter intervals that total 1 to 3 miles—1.6 to 5K—not counting recovery periods.) Warm up and cool down with easy running.

Other training days: Four easy runs of 30 to 60 minutes each.

Rest days: One with no running, but possibly easy cross-training.

Not So Fast

The stranger apologized for calling on a weekend night. "I'll only take a minute of your time," he said, then talked much longer than that.

"You mentioned in an article that one reason for the slowdown in U.S. runners is the 'fun-run factor,'" the caller began. "I'm happy to see your metamorphosis from the person who promoted long slow distance [LSD] to admitting now that you were wrong. I praise you now for having the nerve to renounce it."

Wrong? Did I say that? Renounce? Hardly!

LSD: The Humane Way to Train, published in 1969, sold modestly and fell out of print before the first running boom struck full force in the 1970s. To claim that this thin booklet influenced the course of running for a generation is absurd. However, the name far outlived the booklet. People who talk of LSD today probably never read the original and don't know what I didn't say.

TRAINING TIP

Focus your training program on the long run, which far exceeds everyday training distance. The frequency and maximum length will vary according to your goals, but long runs are equally important for everyone.

All six runners featured in the booklet improved our race times with the LSD approach, but this came as a pleasant surprise. I now see that the improvement probably didn't come from any inherent magic in slower running but because it was *easier* running. It let us freshen up between hard efforts and look forward to the races as actual and figurative changes of pace rather than dread them as more of the same. In this way LSD was less a training system than a *recovery* system. We raced better by staying healthier and happier, not by training harder.

Date _____ **Plans** _____

Training Session

Type of run   ☐ long   ☐ fast   ☐ easy   ☐ none   ☐ race

Distance _____ **Time** _____

Pace _____ per mile   _____ per kilometer

Splits _____ / _____ / _____ / _____ / _____ / _____

Effort   ☐ max   ☐ hard   ☐ moderate   ☐ easy   ☐ rest

Training heart rates   target _____   actual _____

Warm-up _____ **Cool-down** _____ **Cross-training** _____

Training Conditions

Location _____ **Time of day** _____

People   ☐ alone   ☐ with group   ☐ race   ☐ with partner _____

name

Surface   ☐ road   ☐ trail   ☐ track   ☐ mixed _____

Terrain   ☐ flat   ☐ hilly   ☐ mixed _____

Weather _____ **Shoes worn** _____

Diet   drinks during run _____   foods during run _____

Training Rating

Success level   10   9   8   7   6   5   4   3   2   1   0

Training Comments

_____

_____

_____

LSD Lives On

My booklet *Long Slow Distance* never advised taking this form of LSD in pure form (that is, nothing but long and slow). All six featured runners went fast sometimes, if only in frequent short races. The fast running, taken in small amounts, made LSD work.

The booklet's main weakness was in its title. It suggested running as long as possible at the slowest possible pace. Only two of the runners profiled there topped 100 miles (160K) a week habitually. They happened to be the fastest two, 1968 Boston Marathon winner Amby Burfoot and Bob Deines, Olympic Trials Marathon fourth-placer that same year.

The other four runners averaged what would now be fairly modest distances of 50 to 80 miles (80 to 120K) a week. We ran what would now be a relatively brisk pace of seven to eight minutes a mile (4-1/2 to 5 per kilometer).

Shortly after publication of *Long Slow Distance*, I quit using that misleading term. I preferred the less catchy but more descriptive *gentle running*, modest in length and pace. One good test for the value of any practice is how long it lasts. If it doesn't work well, it vanishes. If worthwhile, it endures.

The message in the *Long Slow Distance* booklet must have had some value. Many of us still run this way, no matter what we choose to call it. Critics still say of LSD that "all it ever did was develop long slow runners." In reply I say that it is far better to be a slow runner than *no* runner.

TRAINING TIP

With the marathon in sight you've already started adding distance to your long run. Now ask yourself this: How much farther do I need to go, and how can I go that far without running into trouble?

Date _____ *Plans* _____

Training Session

Type of run ☐ long ☐ fast ☐ easy ☐ none ☐ race

Distance _____ *Time* _____

Pace _____ per mile _____ per kilometer

Splits _____ / _____ / _____ / _____ / _____ / _____

Effort ☐ max ☐ hard ☐ moderate ☐ easy ☐ rest

Training heart rates target _____ actual _____

Warm-up _____ *Cool-down* _____ *Cross-training* _____

Training Conditions

Location _____ *Time of day* _____

People ☐ alone ☐ with group ☐ race ☐ with partner _____
_{name}

Surface ☐ road ☐ trail ☐ track ☐ mixed _____

Terrain ☐ flat ☐ hilly ☐ mixed _____

Weather _____ *Shoes worn* _____

Diet drinks during run _____ foods during run _____

Training Rating

Success level 10 9 8 7 6 5 4 3 2 1 0

Training Comments

_____

_____

_____

Wall Climbing

Brian McGrath's path might never have crossed mine if he hadn't attended the Napa Valley Marathon's breakfast with authors. I got to know most of these few guests, and none better than Brian, a software executive from Houston.

We talked in Napa about his running concerns. (I even convinced him to try walking breaks the next day.) This discussion has continued through e-mail.

"In my last two marathons—Las Vegas and Napa Valley—I was doing well into about 21 to 22 miles [33 to 35K], then hit the wall and slowed significantly—particularly in Napa," he said in his first note. So much for walks lowering or demolishing his wall.

"Can you suggest any training techniques to avoid this?" Brian wrote. "It is frustrating to be strong going through 20 miles [32K] then slow by two minutes per mile [more than a minute per kilometer]."

TRAINING TIP

Aim to run at least two-thirds of the marathon distance (at least 17 miles or 28K) before race day. Three-fourths (20 miles or 32K) or more is an even better goal, since each extra step beyond the minimum adds assurance of finishing the race.

I replied that wall hitting nearly always happens for one of two reasons, or both combined: long runs too short, or early pace too fast. Then I asked for his long-run history before these two marathons. His answer would help me frame mine.

He listed three marathons and a 50K, all in less than three months. "Plus I had long runs of 18 to 21 miles about every other week," he noted.

Brian's response brought up a third possibility (besides too-short long runs and too-fast starts) that I'd overlooked. This was being a little more tired when he started each of the marathons.

Date _____ *Plans* _____

Training Session

Type of run   □ long   □ fast   □ easy   □ none   □ race

Distance _____ *Time* _____

Pace _____ per mile   _____ per kilometer

Splits _____ / _____ / _____ / _____ / _____ / _____

Effort   □ max   □ hard   □ moderate   □ easy   □ rest

Training heart rates target _____ actual _____

Warm-up _____ *Cool-down* _____ *Cross-training* _____

Training Conditions

Location _____ *Time of day* _____

People □ alone   □ with group   □ race   □ with partner _____
                                                                name

Surface   □ road   □ trail   □ track   □ mixed _____

Terrain   □ flat   □ hilly   □ mixed _____

Weather _____ *Shoes worn* _____

Diet   drinks during run _____   foods during run _____

Training Rating

Success level   10   9   8   7   6   5   4   3   2   1   0

Training Comments

_____

_____

_____

═══ Avoiding the Wall ═══

When marathoner Brian McGrath reported hitting the wall in his recent frequent marathons, I told him that his schedule of three races at this distance plus a 50K in the past three months had been too ambitious. "You never allowed more than four weeks between these races. So it shouldn't be too surprising that fatigue caught up with you in the late miles."

I added that the old one-easy-day-per-race-mile rule of recovery really works. It translates to allowing about a month after a marathon with nothing long or fast, and definitely no racing. One day per *kilometer* might work even better, which means six easy weeks to shake off the effects of a marathon.

Brian came back with another question: "Should my long training runs be more than 22 miles, maybe 26 or 30 [35, 42, or 48K] so that my legs will know the full distance?" My reply: His marathons themselves had qualified as his long runs of late, averaging one every three to four weeks. He needed no others of full length.

Brian's next marathon, at Rotterdam, came six weeks after Napa Valley. For him this qualified as an extended vacation. His report: "I felt that Rotterdam was one of the best marathons I have run. I finished the last 5 miles [8K] really strong. I stopped for water at the 40K [25-mile] mark and almost sprinted from there."

TRAINING TIP

Take your long run about one minute per mile (or a little less than one minute per kilometer) slower than projected marathon time. At faster paces these runs become too much like the race itself—and require long recovery periods that interrupt regular training.

Any marathon you finish feeling strong is a good one, no matter what the clock reads.

Date _____ *Plans* _____

Training Session

Type of run ☐ long   ☐ fast   ☐ easy   ☐ none   ☐ race

Distance _____ **Time** _____

Pace _____ per mile   _____ per kilometer

Splits _____ / _____ / _____ / _____ / _____ / _____

Effort ☐ max   ☐ hard   ☐ moderate   ☐ easy   ☐ rest

Training heart rates target _____ actual _____

Warm-up _____ **Cool-down** _____ **Cross-training** _____

Training Conditions

Location _____ **Time of day** _____

People ☐ alone   ☐ with group   ☐ race   ☐ with partner _____
name

Surface ☐ road   ☐ trail   ☐ track   ☐ mixed _____

Terrain ☐ flat   ☐ hilly   ☐ mixed _____

Weather _____ **Shoes worn** _____

Diet drinks during run _____   foods during run _____

Training Rating

Success level   10   9   8   7   6   5   4   3   2   1   0

Training Comments

_____

_____

_____

How Long to Run?

Let's say that a marathon looms on your distant horizon, a full training program away. Let's say also that you accept the long run as the centerpiece of this program, trusting it to take you where you want to go. But you're still asking, How long? How fast? How often? You'll find almost as many answers as there are training plans. These are my answers.

How long? First, draw your start and finish lines for training. In the beginning, don't let your ambition outpace your ability. Run no more than 2 miles (3K) beyond the length of your recent longest run.

Wherever you start, aim to reach 20 miles (32K) in this program. You've heard this figure before because it works. Going this distance builds confidence along with fitness. By running this far, you rehearse most of what a marathon has to offer. This is only about three-fourths of a marathon. Where, you might wonder if you aren't already a marathoner, will the extra 10 kilometers come from if you haven't trained that far? It comes from the magic of race day. That day brings soul-stirring conditions that you can't duplicate on solo and small-group training runs.

TRAINING TIP

Increase the length of your long runs by about 2 miles (3K) each time. This gives you a sense of progress without overwhelming your ability to take each of the new steps at one- to three-week intervals.

The excitement carries you many extra miles or kilometers, but not an unlimited number. If you train yourself to 20 miles (32K), the race-day effect will take you the rest of the way. Neglect your homework, however, and even the adrenaline rush will run out before the distance does.

Date _____ *Plans* _____

Training Session

Type of run   ☐ long   ☐ fast   ☐ easy   ☐ none   ☐ race

Distance _____   *Time* _____

Pace _____ per mile   _____ per kilometer

Splits _____ / _____ / _____ / _____ / _____ / _____

Effort   ☐ max   ☐ hard   ☐ moderate   ☐ easy   ☐ rest

Training heart rates target _____   actual _____

Warm-up _____   **Cool-down** _____   **Cross-training** _____

Training Conditions

Location _____   **Time of day** _____

People   ☐ alone   ☐ with group   ☐ race   ☐ with partner _____
name

Surface   ☐ road   ☐ trail   ☐ track   ☐ mixed _____

Terrain   ☐ flat   ☐ hilly   ☐ mixed _____

Weather _____   **Shoes worn** _____

Diet   drinks during run _____   foods during run _____

Training Rating

Success level   10   9   8   7   6   5   4   3   2   1   0

Training Comments

_____

_____

_____

How Fast to Run Long?

Shaping my answer is my first experience with a marathon. My longest run was 20 miles (32K). Its pace was eight-minute miles (five-minute kilometers). The race averaged 1-1/2 minutes per mile (one minute per kilometer) faster than the training run.

The longest training run had taken the same amount of time as the marathon. I'd trained to spend that long on my feet, even while running a shorter distance. Later I upped the pace in training, but never again raced a faster marathon.

How fast? The training run is not a race. Treat it as one, and you may recover too slowly from one long run to the next. Full recovery from "races" this long takes most runners several weeks, and you don't have that long to wait between these training runs. So instead of pushing the pace, focus on upping your distance. Back well off from the fastest you could run.

TRAINING TIP

Reach maximum training distance in the 10th week of this program. This gives you three weeks to recover before the marathon, which assures you that you'll go into the race healthy, fresh, and eager.

Train one to two minutes per mile (about a minute per kilometer) slower than you could race this same distance. You could surprise yourself by running that much faster on marathon day than you'd trained, even at the longer distance. Again, credit the race-day magic.

While you're at it, credit your training. If you backed well away from race pace, you covered much less than full marathon distance but ran almost the full amount of time that the race would take. You were ready to spend this much time on your feet again, but moving them faster.

Date _____ *Plans* _____

Training Session

Type of run ☐ long   ☐ fast   ☐ easy   ☐ none   ☐ race

Distance _____   *Time* _____

Pace _____ per mile   _____ per kilometer

Splits _____ / _____ / _____ / _____ / _____ / _____

Effort ☐ max   ☐ hard   ☐ moderate   ☐ easy   ☐ rest

Training heart rates target _____   actual _____

Warm-up _____   *Cool-down* _____   *Cross-training* _____

Training Conditions

Location _____   *Time of day* _____

People ☐ alone   ☐ with group   ☐ race   ☐ with partner _____
name

Surface ☐ road   ☐ trail   ☐ track   ☐ mixed _____

Terrain ☐ flat   ☐ hilly   ☐ mixed _____

Weather _____   *Shoes worn* _____

Diet drinks during run _____   foods during run _____

Training Rating

Success level   10   9   8   7   6   5   4   3   2   1   0

Training Comments

_____

_____

_____

How Often to Run Long?

Arthur Lydiard gave us the long run in the 1960s. The success of his New Zealand runners made the long run a weekly practice of runners everywhere.

Once a week may have worked well for the young elite, but it proved to be too often to run far for runners who recovered slowly. I was one who needed more time between.

How often? If the question means how often to run a particular distance, the answer is once. Runners like having a sense of progression, so make a steady march up in long-run distances without repeating any of them.

The steps themselves are small. They progress from shortest to longest by 2 miles (3K) at a time. With these runs requiring ever-bigger efforts, and therefore ever-longer recoveries, they're best not taken weekly but only every second or third weekend.

Set the program's length by where you start. An 8-mile (13K) beginning leads to a three- to four-month program. A half-marathon start can shrink the program to as little as two months. The longest run before the marathon is the last and hardest one. Place it at least three weeks before the race; a full month is better.

What to do between long runs? Recover from the last one and recharge for the next one with mostly easy running. When one part of the training program (the long run) goes way up in effort, another (the remaining days) must come down in compensation. Shorter runs help make the longer ones work.

TRAINING TIP

View each of your long runs as a dress rehearsal of the marathon. Run on the race course if possible, or at least mimic its terrain. Test the shoes and clothing you'll wear on race day, and test the foods and drinks you'll take then.

Date _____ *Plans* _____

Training Session

Type of run ☐ long ☐ fast ☐ easy ☐ none ☐ race

Distance _____ *Time* _____

Pace _____ per mile _____ per kilometer

Splits _____ / _____ / _____ / _____ / _____ / _____

Effort ☐ max ☐ hard ☐ moderate ☐ easy ☐ rest

Training heart rates target _____ actual _____

Warm-up _____ *Cool-down* _____ *Cross-training* _____

Training Conditions

Location _____ *Time of day* _____

People ☐ alone ☐ with group ☐ race ☐ with partner _____
name

Surface ☐ road ☐ trail ☐ track ☐ mixed _____

Terrain ☐ flat ☐ hilly ☐ mixed _____

Weather _____ *Shoes worn* _____

Diet drinks during run _____ foods during run _____

Training Rating

Success level   10   9   8   7   6   5   4   3   2   1   0

Training Comments

_____

_____

_____

A few speedsters drink on the run. You may need, and want, to pause at aid stations and to take other planned walking breaks.

TAKING BREAKS

Walking breaks are standard in the Cruiser program, but they can help Pacers and even Racers who might be having trouble extending their long runs or recovering quickly from them. The recommended mix: Run about a mile (1.6K), then walk about a minute before running again. Think of this as interval training for long distances. Choose your program from the options listed, assign runs to the next seven days of diary pages, and add details there for completed training.

Cruiser Program

Big day: Long run of 14 to 16 miles (22 to 25K), or about a 2-mile (3K) increase from your last one. Mix running and walking while covering the distance no faster than your projected marathon pace.

Other training days: Three or four easy runs of 30 to 45 minutes each, with walking breaks optional.

Rest days: Two or three with no running, but possibly easy cross-training.

Pacer Program

Big day: Race of 5K to 10K, or fast solo run of 1 to 3 miles (1.6 to 5K; may be broken into intervals) at current 10K race pace. Warm up and cool down with easy running.

Other training days: Four or five easy runs of 30 to 60 minutes each.

Rest days: One or two with no running, but possibly easy cross-training.

Racer Program

Long day: Long run of 16 to 18 miles (26 to 29K), or about a 2-mile (3K) increase from the last one. Run about one minute per mile (35 seconds per kilometer) slower than marathon pace.

Fast day: 1- to 3-mile run (1.6 to 5K) at current 10K race pace. (This may be broken into shorter intervals that total 1 to 3 miles—1.6 to 5K—not counting recovery periods.) Warm up and cool down with easy running.

Other training days: Four easy runs of 30 to 60 minutes each.

Rest days: One with no running, but possibly easy cross-training.

Talking the Walk

Real runners never walk, you say? I used to think so myself, but not anymore. Talking down walking ended for me in the 1970s. Before that I was a typical "real runner." You know the type—runs in circles at stoplights rather than take one walking step.

Then reports began reaching me about ultrarunners greatly extending their distance range by taking planned rest breaks. The practice struck me as really weird in 1971, but I wasn't above experimenting with weird ideas.

TRAINING TIP

If the distances and progress rates quoted for long runs sound imposing, ease the efforts by adopting the technique of intermittent running. For each mile or kilometer you run, stop and walk for about a minute.

The first test made a believer of me. I entered a 100-mile (160K) race, stopped for a few minutes every 5 miles (8K) early on, more often later, and reached 70 miles (113K) before dropping out. My mind betrayed me before my body did. Seeing no one else on the course at two o'clock in the morning, I could find no persuasive reason to continue.

"Why quit now?" said the lone race official. "You only have 30 miles [48K] to go."

My race was a failure for not finishing, but it was a great eye opener in another way. This 70 miles doubled my previous longest distance. Plus the pace was faster than I could have run steadily (in the highly unlikely event I could have run this far without stopping). And recovery came much faster than it ever had after much shorter but uninterrupted races.

I've praised and promoted walking for runners ever since. And I've defended its good name against critics who claim that walk breaks make runs less real.

Date _____ *Plans* _____

Training Session

Type of run ☐ long ☐ fast ☐ easy ☐ none ☐ race

Distance _____ *Time* _____

Pace _____ per mile _____ per kilometer

Splits _____ / _____ / _____ / _____ / _____ / _____

Effort ☐ max ☐ hard ☐ moderate ☐ easy ☐ rest

Training heart rates target _____ actual _____

Warm-up _____ *Cool-down* _____ *Cross-training* _____

Training Conditions

Location _____ *Time of day* _____

People ☐ alone ☐ with group ☐ race ☐ with partner _____
name

Surface ☐ road ☐ trail ☐ track ☐ mixed _____

Terrain ☐ flat ☐ hilly ☐ mixed _____

Weather _____ *Shoes worn* _____

Diet drinks during run _____ foods during run _____

Training Rating

Success level 10 9 8 7 6 5 4 3 2 1 0

Training Comments

_____

_____

_____

Walking Isn't Cheating

In certain running circles, among some runners who call themselves "serious," walk is a four-letter word. Reacting to the growing popularity of walk breaks and their primary promoter Jeff Galloway, some purist runners have taken to equating this practice with cheating. They claim that interrupting runs with walks is only for the untalented and undedicated.

If you're tempted to think that walking is wimping out, consider who does this and why. The benefits and beauties of running's closest cousin are many and varied:

- Adding distance. Walk breaks came down to marathoners from above, from ultrarunners such as Tom Osler. He was among the first writers to speak well of this practice, saying in 1978 in his *Serious Runner's Handbook* that well-placed walks would instantly double the distance anyone could run nonstop.

- Adding speed. This is the traditional use of interval training—breaking the run into faster segments with brief rests in between. My friend and fellow writer Bernie Greene from Maryland switched to shorter, faster training with walk breaks because the intervals eased his chronic knee pain. Within six months his 5K race time dropped from 25 to 20 minutes.

TRAINING TIP

Look at the payoffs: You can instantly double the length of your longest nonstop running distance by adding walking breaks. You can also maintain a faster pace for the running portions and recover more quickly.

- Easing efforts. Even the easiest steady run might not be easy enough. Interspersing walks can speed recovery from the hardest racing and training and from injury or illness. It also can make chronic pain more tolerable. This happened with another friend of mine, Tim Zbikowski from Minnesota, whose arthritic hip reacted much better to run-walk than to run-every-step.

Date _____ **Plans** _____

Training Session

Type of run ☐ long   ☐ fast   ☐ easy   ☐ none   ☐ race

Distance _____   **Time** _____

Pace _____ per mile   _____ per kilometer

Splits _____ / _____ / _____ / _____ / _____ / _____

Effort ☐ max   ☐ hard   ☐ moderate   ☐ easy   ☐ rest

Training heart rates target _____   actual _____

Warm-up _____ **Cool-down** _____ **Cross-training** _____

Training Conditions

Location _____   **Time of day** _____

People ☐ alone   ☐ with group   ☐ race   ☐ with partner _____

name

Surface   ☐ road   ☐ trail   ☐ track   ☐ mixed _____

Terrain   ☐ flat   ☐ hilly   ☐ mixed _____

Weather _____   **Shoes worn** _____

Diet drinks during run _____   foods during run _____

Training Rating

Success level   10   9   8   7   6   5   4   3   2   1   0

Training Comments

_____

_____

_____

Why Walk?

More good reasons to add walks to your runs, or walking in lieu of running:

- Beginning or returning. New and lapsed runners advance quickly and safely by mixing walks into their runs—or, at first, by adding short runs to what's still mostly a walk. I suggest to my college-age running students that newcomers start with as little as one-minute runs separated by five-minute walks.

- Warming up and cooling down. We see all manner of fancy exercises for doing both. Perhaps the best is the simplest: Walk a few minutes before and after each run. Some of America's best young runners, those at Stanford University, habitually walk their first quarter-mile (400 meters) each day. This eases the transition from resting to running, and walking works just as well later for the reverse, run-to-rest shift.

- Substituting and supplementing. Walking is an effective, if too often overlooked, cross-training activity. Two months before his 77th birthday, John Keston became the oldest marathoner to break 3-1/2 hours, running 3:22:59. His training: Run 14 to 17 miles (22 to 27K) every third day, with 5- to 6-mile (8 to 10K) walks the other days.

TRAINING TIP

If you don't like the word *walk*, think of it as another application of interval training. Intervals break a large chunk of work into smaller pieces to make the total task more manageable.

- Replacing running. We can't all keep running forever. Ted Corbitt couldn't. When severe asthma stopped the Olympian's running, he switched to long-distance walking. At age 82, he walked a six-day race and averaged 50 miles (80K) daily. Corbitt could have adopted other activities, but he found that walking most closely matched the earth-below, sky-above feelings of a good run.

Date _____ *Plans* _____

Training Session

Type of run □ long □ fast □ easy □ none □ race

Distance _____ *Time* _____

Pace _____ per mile _____ per kilometer

Splits _____ / _____ / _____ / _____ / _____ / _____

Effort □ max □ hard □ moderate □ easy □ rest

Training heart rates target _____ actual _____

Warm-up _____ *Cool-down* _____ *Cross-training* _____

Training Conditions

Location _____ *Time of day* _____

People □ alone □ with group □ race □ with partner _____
name

Surface □ road □ trail □ track □ mixed _____

Terrain □ flat □ hilly □ mixed _____

Weather _____ *Shoes worn* _____

Diet drinks during run _____ foods during run _____

Training Rating

Success level   10   9   8   7   6   5   4   3   2   1   0

Training Comments

_____

_____

_____

Every Minute Counts

Several pet themes of mine converged in a letter from reader Steve Vaughan from Ohio. He bought into the ideas of adding walking breaks to some runs and of running by time periods instead of distances. He also agreed with my suggestion of keeping records by the month instead of by the week. And he accepted quoting the average length of daily runs instead of a monthly grand total.

Steve then said that I still had some explaining to do. He asked, "Do you include the minutes spent in the walking breaks into total time for logging minutes?"

Good, simple question. Long answer to follow.

TRAINING TIP

Pacers and Racers, use the walking breaks primarily as a training option. You can aim to eliminate the breaks on race day, when the excitement of the event probably should make walking unnecessary.

Walking breaks are now an occasional option for me. I don't always exercise it, but I don't hesitate to walk if needed—especially when the runs grow long or when I'm recovering from some race or malady.

These breaks, averaging a minute or so in every 10, can make the long runs longer by stretching available energy. They can make the fast runs faster with rest breaks after the warm-up and between intervals. And they can make the easy run easier through intermittent rather than constant pounding on sore or weary legs.

With these benefits in mind, I sometimes walk in short runs and long, alone and in crowds as large as 31,000 while feeling no shame. The question today, though, isn't whether to walk or not. It's how to deal with the walk time. I now say that every minute counts toward the total.

Date _____ *Plans* _____

Training Session

Type of run   ☐ long   ☐ fast   ☐ easy   ☐ none   ☐ race

Distance _____   *Time* _____

Pace _____ per mile   _____ per kilometer

Splits _____ / _____ / _____ / _____ / _____ / _____

Effort   ☐ max   ☐ hard   ☐ moderate   ☐ easy   ☐ rest

Training heart rates target _____ actual _____

Warm-up _____   *Cool-down* _____   *Cross-training* _____

Training Conditions

Location _____   *Time of day* _____

People ☐ alone   ☐ with group   ☐ race   ☐ with partner _____
name

Surface   ☐ road   ☐ trail   ☐ track   ☐ mixed _____

Terrain   ☐ flat   ☐ hilly   ☐ mixed _____

Weather _____   *Shoes worn* _____

Diet drinks during run _____   foods during run _____

Training Rating

Success level   10   9   8   7   6   5   4   3   2   1   0

Training Comments

_____

_____

_____

Keeping Time

I once punched off the watch with the first walking step, clocking in again only as the run resumed. It didn't feel quite right to say that I'd *run* an hour when it was really a run-*walk*. This offended my journalistic scruples, as did making up a word—*ralk*? *wun*?—to describe the mix.

Then I confessed in writing to this habit of keeping walking minutes off the watch. I told whimsically about running 3:30 in a marathon—but needing 3:56 to finish it. The extra time was spent walking. This story brought howls of protest from several readers. They called this way of keeping score "cheating."

TRAINING TIP

Cruisers, you can plan to continue taking walking breaks during the marathon. If your only goal is to cover the distance, use any trick that will take you to the finish line—and this trick is one of the most useful.

In fact, I never seriously claimed the lower time as official in this or any other race. But all training runs were by time periods, at unknown distances, and the walking minutes were kept off the watch.

Reaction to my article made me question the honesty of this practice. Sufficiently shamed, I mended my record-keeping ways. The clock immediately began ticking through all the breaks, and into my diary went only the total run-plus-walk time. This practice continues today, with the watch starting at the first running step of the day and ending on the last.

The breaks aren't running, to be sure. In the name of honesty and accuracy I take care to say I've "done" or "finished" a long race, not "run" it.

Yet the walks aren't time apart from the run but are an investment in it. They deserve full recognition for their contributions.

Date _____ **Plans** _____

Training Session

Type of run   ☐ long   ☐ fast   ☐ easy   ☐ none   ☐ race

Distance _____   **Time** _____

Pace _____ per mile   _____ per kilometer

Splits _____ / _____ / _____ / _____ / _____ / _____

Effort   ☐ max   ☐ hard   ☐ moderate   ☐ easy   ☐ rest

Training heart rates target _____   actual _____

Warm-up _____ **Cool-down** _____ **Cross-training** _____

Training Conditions

Location _____ **Time of day** _____

People ☐ alone ☐ with group ☐ race ☐ with partner _____
                                                              name

Surface   ☐ road   ☐ trail   ☐ track   ☐ mixed _____

Terrain   ☐ flat   ☐ hilly   ☐ mixed _____

Weather _____   **Shoes worn** _____

Diet   drinks during run _____   foods during run _____

Training Rating

Success level   10   9   8   7   6   5   4   3   2   1   0

Training Comments

_____

_____

_____

Time Travel

Time is precious to any runner. It's how we keep score in this sport, so we glory in every second saved and worry about each one lost in the race against our pace goal. We look with suspicion on anything that complicates the simple matter of checking pace, as seems to happen when taking walking breaks.

Phil Uglow from Toronto likes the idea of taking walking breaks during his long runs. But he wrote, "Could you talk about how to calculate run-walk times into minutes per kilometer or per mile? I train with a number of run-walkers, and they are all baffled—as am I—on how to set various paces."

TRAINING TIP

Don't think you'll sacrifice a lot of time with walking breaks. A one-minute break each mile totals 26 minutes of walking (or one minute for every 2K equals 22 minutes). But you still cover distance while walking and probably net only about 10 minutes lost.

When he contacted me, Uglow and friends were training for a four-hour marathon. They worried, as most new walk-breakers do, about falling behind their intended pace while walking—or at least having the breaks play havoc with their splits.

Another good reason for letting the time "run" on during walks, I told Uglow, is that it simplifies split taking and pacing. If you think it's a complication to include walk breaks in total time, think how confusing it becomes if you punch out during the breaks.

I recommended that he not check his pace at the usual 1-kilometer or 1-mile intervals. Some kilometers and miles might include two breaks and others none. Instead, take splits at longer intervals such as every 5 kilometers to 5 miles (8K). This equalizes the number of walks per timing period and gives a truer picture of how the pace is going.

Date _____ *Plans* _____

Training Session

Type of run   □ long   □ fast   □ easy   □ none   □ race

Distance _____   **Time** _____

Pace _____ per mile   _____ per kilometer

Splits _____ / _____ / _____ / _____ / _____ / _____

Effort   □ max   □ hard   □ moderate   □ easy   □ rest

Training heart rates target _____   actual _____

Warm-up _____   **Cool-down** _____   **Cross-training** _____

Training Conditions

Location _____   **Time of day** _____

People   □ alone   □ with group   □ race   □ with partner _____
name

Surface   □ road   □ trail   □ track   □ mixed _____

Terrain   □ flat   □ hilly   □ mixed _____

Weather _____   **Shoes worn** _____

Diet drinks during run _____   foods during run _____

Training Rating

Success level   10   9   8   7   6   5   4   3   2   1   0

Training Comments

_____

_____

_____

Time Lost and Saved

Brief walking breaks cost less time than you might imagine. If you walk for one minute in every mile (1.6K), how much time do you think you'd lose against someone who runs nonstop? Your first guess might be a minute per mile. That would be the right answer only if you screeched to a dead stop during the breaks. But remember that you're still moving at about half your running pace, so this cuts your overall slowdown to about 30 seconds per mile (slightly more for the fastest runners, slightly less for the slowest). Realize too that the walks affect your running pace in two good ways:

1. Run-walkers tend to go slightly faster in the run segments than if they tried to run without pause. Notice the people beside you who don't stop as you take your break. You're likely to catch right back up to them as you resume running . . . and leave them behind as the distance adds up.

2. Run-walkers tend to hold their pace longer (or even increase it), while nonstop runners are more likely to meet a wall sooner. The walks also act as leg savers and energy extenders, which help you avoid a time-wasting slowdown late in a run or race.

The longer the distance, the less the difference in pace between run-walking and run-every-stepping. A four-hour marathoner might lose no time at all by taking breaks. He or she might even save some precious seconds per mile—which multiply into minutes in a marathon.

TRAINING TIP

If you opt to walk in the marathon, plan to do so at each of the drink stations—usually spaced 2 or 3 miles (3 to 5K) apart. This ensures that you'll swallow the drinks instead of gagging on them.

Date _____ *Plans* _____

Training Session

Type of run   ☐ long   ☐ fast   ☐ easy   ☐ none   ☐ race

Distance _____   *Time* _____

Pace _____ per mile   _____ per kilometer

Splits _____ / _____ / _____ / _____ / _____ / _____

Effort   ☐ max   ☐ hard   ☐ moderate   ☐ easy   ☐ rest

Training heart rates target _____ actual _____

Warm-up _____ *Cool-down* _____ *Cross-training* _____

Training Conditions

Location _____   *Time of day* _____

People ☐ alone   ☐ with group   ☐ race   ☐ with partner _____
                                                              name

Surface   ☐ road   ☐ trail   ☐ track   ☐ mixed _____

Terrain   ☐ flat   ☐ hilly   ☐ mixed _____

Weather _____   *Shoes worn* _____

Diet   drinks during run _____   foods during run _____

Training Rating

Success level   10   9   8   7   6   5   4   3   2   1   0

Training Comments

_____

_____

_____

One way to keep from hitting the wall is to train long enough. The other is to pace yourself realistically and evenly.

SETTING PACE

We've talked about projected marathon pace. But how do you project what you'll run? Get out a calculator and multiply your most recent half-marathon time by 2.3 (for Cruisers), 2.2 (for Pacers), or 2.1 (for Racers). For instance, 1:50 times 2.3 equals a potential marathon time of 4:13, or a little under 10 minutes per mile (6 minutes per kilometer). "Predicting Your Time" on page 241 puts these calculations in table form. "Pacing Your Marathon" on page 242 determines your ideal race pace based on the time forecast. Choose your program from the options listed, assign runs to the next seven days of diary pages, and add details there for completed training.

Cruiser Program

Big day: Semilong run of 7 to 8 miles (11 to 13K), or half the distance of last week's long one. Run this distance nonstop, with no walking breaks. Run slightly faster than your projected marathon pace.

Other training days: Three or four easy runs of 30 to 45 minutes each, with walking breaks optional.

Rest days: Two or three with no running, but possibly easy cross-training.

Pacer Program

Big day: Long run of 16 to 18 miles (26 to 29K), or about a 2-mile (3K) increase from your last one. Walking breaks optional. Run about one minute per mile (35 seconds per kilometer) slower than your projected marathon pace.

Other training days: Four or five easy runs of 30 to 60 minutes each.

Rest days: One or two with no running, but possibly easy cross-training.

Racer Program

Long day: Long run of 18 to 20 miles (29 to 32K), or about a 2-mile (3K) increase from the last one. Run about one minute per mile (35 seconds per kilometer) slower than marathon pace.

Fast day: 1- to 3-mile (1.6 to 5K) run at current 10K race pace. (This may be broken into shorter intervals that total 1 to 3 miles—1.6 to 5K—not counting recovery periods.) Warm up and cool down with easy running.

Other training days: Four easy runs of 30 to 60 minutes each.

Rest days: One with no running, but possibly easy cross-training.

Relaxed Pace

One of the most basic tenets of running training is also a hard one to sell to ambitious, impatient runners. It's that you must run less than your best most of the time. Put another way, you can't go all out all the time. Maximum efforts are prescription items, best taken in small and well-spaced doses. Put yet another way, you must pace yourself. Find what your limits are in races, then back well away from them on all but a few of your runs.

The hardest runs are challenging and exciting but also temporarily damaging. The easier ones repair the damage and bring you back stronger for the next challenge. Assuming that you accept this premise, the trick is knowing how much less than your best to run most of the time. What pace is easy enough to hold day after day but not too easy to give you a training benefit? Where is your building zone, and where is your comfort zone?

The modern way to measure effort is to monitor your heart rate, running at a certain percentage of your maximum. The time-tested method is to drive your training routes in a car, stepping out to mark the mile points.

There's a much simpler way to settle into a pace that's right for you. It works just as well as wearing a heart-rate monitor or timing every mile—and sometimes better. That is to relax during most runs and just let whatever happens to the pace happen.

The pace that feels right is right. It feels neither too fast nor too slow, no matter what the watch reads.

TRAINING TIP

Simulate the marathon distance in long runs but at a slower pace. Mimic racing pace in your fast runs, but only at a shorter distance. Combine full distance at full pace only when it counts: in the race itself.

Date _____ *Plans* _____

Training Session

Type of run   □ long   □ fast   □ easy   □ none   □ race

Distance _____   *Time* _____

Pace _____ per mile   _____ per kilometer

Splits _____ / _____ / _____ / _____ / _____ / _____

Effort   □ max   □ hard   □ moderate   □ easy   □ rest

Training heart rates target _____ actual _____

Warm-up _____ *Cool-down* _____ *Cross-training* _____

Training Conditions

Location _____ *Time of day* _____

People □ alone □ with group □ race □ with partner _____
name

Surface   □ road   □ trail   □ track   □ mixed _____

Terrain   □ flat   □ hilly   □ mixed _____

Weather _____ *Shoes worn* _____

Diet drinks during run _____ foods during run _____

Training Rating

Success level   10   9   8   7   6   5   4   3   2   1   0

Training Comments

_____

_____

_____

Taking Your Time

Backing off the pace was the guiding principle in my first book. Its title, *Long Slow Distance*, seemed to promote running the slowest possible pace. A better word than *slow* would have been *relaxed*.

Relaxing meant setting no time goals on most runs, checking no splits, accepting whatever pace the day's feelings and conditions allowed. My comfort zone settled at one to two minutes per mile (or about one minute per kilometer) slower than my current racing rate for that same distance.

Today, more than three decades further along, I can't race any distance as fast as my slowest training once was. But the plus-one to plus-two-per-mile gap between relaxed pace and racing pace remains constant.

How to relax and let body wisdom find the right pace for the day? Run by time periods while leaving distances unchecked, or run known distances but leave the watch at home. Either way protects you from racing yourself in training.

I prefer the time-only approach simply because it's more practical. You needn't measure a course nor stick to a plotted route. Time passes at the same rate wherever you run it. The big advantage of running by time is that you can't hurry it, so you settle into a pace that makes the time pass most pleasantly.

TRAINING TIP

Complement your long runs with some that are semilong. These let you know how it feels to run at marathon pace for an extended distance while still not overwhelming you with their length and degree of difficulty.

A compromise between the two approaches allows for both a known distance and a watch. But to keep the pressure off, you take no splits and keep no training-course records.

Date _____ **Plans** _____

Training Session

Type of run   ☐ long   ☐ fast   ☐ easy   ☐ none   ☐ race

Distance _____ **Time** _____

Pace _____ per mile   _____ per kilometer

Splits _____ / _____ / _____ / _____ / _____ / _____

Effort   ☐ max   ☐ hard   ☐ moderate   ☐ easy   ☐ rest

Training heart rates   target _____   actual _____

Warm-up _____ **Cool-down** _____ **Cross-training** _____

Training Conditions

Location _____ **Time of day** _____

People   ☐ alone   ☐ with group   ☐ race   ☐ with partner _____

name

Surface   ☐ road   ☐ trail   ☐ track   ☐ mixed _____

Terrain   ☐ flat   ☐ hilly   ☐ mixed _____

Weather _____ **Shoes worn** _____

Diet   drinks during run _____   foods during run _____

Training Rating

Success level   10   9   8   7   6   5   4   3   2   1   0

Training Comments

_____

_____

_____

Acing the Pacing

Students in the beginning racing classes I teach like to know both their distance and time. At their age and stage of running it's difficult to sell them on listening to the body instead of eyeing the watch.

They want to know how fast they're going, and many of them want to race every longer and "easier" run. To reinforce the idea of *not* pushing limits here, I give a daily "Pace Ace" award for the runner who comes closest to his or her target time. That target is one minute per mile (about 35 seconds per kilometer) slower than current 5K race pace. It's an easy figure to remember and calculate, and I'm happy if they agree to back off their race pace even by that much.

Another hard sell to young runners is the concept that pace means more than per-mile or per-kilometer averages on today's run. It also means pacing from one day to the next and the next and . . .

TRAINING TIP

Between long runs take some that are about half the distance of the latest long session. If you've just run 20 miles (32K), for instance, do 10 miles (16K) this time—but at your projected marathon pace or slightly faster.

Some students complain that the runs I give them feel too easy. I try to tell them that one run doesn't stand alone. Then I ask, "Could you come back tomorrow and run this same one again? Could you run this way three to six days a week, month after month, for years on end, and never tire of it?"

A view of pace that takes you through one run also gets you through dozens or hundreds or thousands of runs. Doing less than your best most of the time keeps you coming back for more. The more you want to come back, the more often you come back, and the more committed runner you become.

Date _____ *Plans* _____

Training Session

Type of run □ long □ fast □ easy □ none □ race

Distance _____ *Time* _____

Pace _____ per mile _____ per kilometer

Splits _____ / _____ / _____ / _____ / _____ / _____

Effort □ max □ hard □ moderate □ easy □ rest

Training heart rates target _____ actual _____

Warm-up _____ *Cool-down* _____ *Cross-training* _____

Training Conditions

Location _____ *Time of day* _____

People □ alone □ with group □ race □ with partner _____
name

Surface □ road □ trail □ track □ mixed _____

Terrain □ flat □ hilly □ mixed _____

Weather _____ *Shoes worn* _____

Diet drinks during run _____ foods during run _____

Training Rating

Success level   10   9   8   7   6   5   4   3   2   1   0

Training Comments

_____

_____

_____

Hurrying Home

To find one of the great misnomers of our sport, look no further than *negative split*. The term is mathematically correct in that subtracting a faster second half of a run from a slower first half yields a negative number.

But to call finishing faster than you start a *negative* is wrong psychologically. This is one of the most positive experiences a runner can have, and you can have it often. It can happen in your everyday runs and in races.

- Normal runs. Almost all daily runs can be positively "negative." This happens naturally if you let it. You ease into the run, bumping up the pace as you warm up. I often run out-and-back courses, going out for 30 minutes and noting the turnaround time. The return trip of equal distances usually takes only 28 minutes—with no apparent increase in effort. Any run that ends better than it started is a good one.

- Races. Alone on a weekday run, your natural tendency is to start slowly and build into your pace of the day. On race day, however, you naturally try to do the opposite. Mass adrenaline poisoning urges you to join the crowd that's starting unwisely. Your race will end better if you resist that urge and smooth out your efforts, keeping your head while others around you are losing theirs. It's depressing to slow down steadily (with "positive" splits). It's uplifting to hold or increase your pace and to pass the unwise toward the end.

TRAINING TIP

As with the long runs, make each semilong one a marathon rehearsal. Run a similar course at the same time of day, and dress and drink as you would on the actual marathon day.

Date _____ Plans _____

Training Session

Type of run   ☐ long   ☐ fast   ☐ easy   ☐ none   ☐ race

Distance _____   **Time** _____

Pace _____ per mile   _____ per kilometer

Splits _____ / _____ / _____ / _____ / _____ / _____

Effort   ☐ max   ☐ hard   ☐ moderate   ☐ easy   ☐ rest

Training heart rates target _____   actual _____

Warm-up _____ **Cool-down** _____ **Cross-training** _____

Training Conditions

Location _____ **Time of day** _____

People ☐ alone   ☐ with group   ☐ race   ☐ with partner _____
name

Surface   ☐ road   ☐ trail   ☐ track   ☐ mixed _____

Terrain   ☐ flat   ☐ hilly   ☐ mixed _____

Weather _____   **Shoes worn** _____

Diet   drinks during run _____   foods during run _____

Training Rating

Success level   10   9   8   7   6   5   4   3   2   1   0

Training Comments

_____

_____

_____

Fast-Finish Training

You can practice fast finishes by mimicking race speed and effort for part of a day's run. This can aid your final kick, which lasts for a hundred meters or so. But its greater value is in teaching you to make a longer, sustained, more controlled push for home.

Regina Jacobs, who remained a world-class runner into her 40s, often won on her finishing kick. When asked how she stays so quick, she said, "I finish every run fast, even if only speeding up for the last 100 meters. This is a constant reminder to my legs of what they have to do in a race."

Regina's practice is one that everyone who races can use. Run frequently at top racing pace, even if the distance run that way is short.

TRAINING TIP

If you enter races longer than 10K, treat them strictly as semilong training runs instead of serious competitions. If the event is a half-marathon, run it at *marathon* pace and not all out.

A favorite session of mine goes like this: Run 3 miles (about 5K) nonstop. Use the first mile (1.6K) as a warm-up, easing into the run as on any other day.

Then run the second mile about one minute faster than the warm-up. This still isn't much of a stretch. The real effort comes on the final mile, where the pace jumps by another minute (to what I'd expect to hold for an entire 5K).

Sometimes I simply run out easily for 15 minutes, hurry back the same way, and take a final time. It usually falls in the 27s. You might call this "negative-split" training. I think of it as "half-fast," with the last half being the faster one by far.

Date _____ **Plans** _____

Training Session

Type of run   ☐ long   ☐ fast   ☐ easy   ☐ none   ☐ race

Distance _____   **Time** _____

Pace _____ per mile   _____ per kilometer

Splits _____ / _____ / _____ / _____ / _____ / _____

Effort   ☐ max   ☐ hard   ☐ moderate   ☐ easy   ☐ rest

Training heart rates target _____   actual _____

Warm-up _____   **Cool-down** _____   **Cross-training** _____

Training Conditions

Location _____   **Time of day** _____

People   ☐ alone   ☐ with group   ☐ race   ☐ with partner _____
name

Surface   ☐ road   ☐ trail   ☐ track   ☐ mixed _____

Terrain   ☐ flat   ☐ hilly   ☐ mixed _____

Weather _____   **Shoes worn** _____

Diet   drinks during run _____   foods during run _____

Training Rating

Success level   10   9   8   7   6   5   4   3   2   1   0

Training Comments

_____

_____

_____

Get Faster Fast

The quickest way to get faster is to race. Race days are magic. The shared excitement, along with the fear factor, takes you places you couldn't go alone. The racing effect can reward you a dozen or more seconds in a single mile (1.6K), which adds up to a minute or more in a 10K, with further multiplication occurring on out to the marathon.

TRAINING TIP

Practice running at or near marathon pace in some or all of your easy runs. This won't seem very fast or hard when you're averaging less than one-quarter the marathon distance on easy days.

The best training *for* racing *is* racing. That was one of my earliest lessons in running. At the start I was a half-miler, for the simple reason that every runner on the team was a half-miler. We did little else but race that distance several times a week, and my time improved by 25 seconds and landed me in the state meet as a high school freshman.

By my senior year I was a miler, and early that season the state's best miler beat me by a full straightaway. Shocked at my slowness, I took a crash course in speed.

Over the next few weeks I raced 10 times, usually at a half-mile. Result: 18 seconds of improvement in the mile and a 10-second PR in just a month . . . and a win at the state meet over the boy who'd beaten me by 100 yards the month before. I credit this win to the frequent and fast racing with an assist from relaxed recovery runs in between. Later I ran farther, faster, harder on more complicated programs—but never better in a single month than May 1961.

This same concept can help a marathoner improve: use shorter races as your speed training.

Date _____ **Plans** _____

Training Session

Type of run   □ long   □ fast   □ easy   □ none   □ race

Distance _____   **Time** _____

Pace _____ per mile   _____ per kilometer

Splits _____ / _____ / _____ / _____ / _____ / _____

Effort   □ max   □ hard   □ moderate   □ easy   □ rest

Training heart rates   target _____   actual _____

Warm-up _____   **Cool-down** _____   **Cross-training** _____

Training Conditions

Location _____   **Time of day** _____

People   □ alone   □ with group   □ race   □ with partner _____
name

Surface   □ road   □ trail   □ track   □ mixed _____

Terrain   □ flat   □ hilly   □ mixed _____

Weather _____   **Shoes worn** _____

Diet   drinks during run _____   foods during run _____

Training Rating

Success level   10   9   8   7   6   5   4   3   2   1   0

Training Comments

_____

_____

_____

Racing As Training

When praising racing as training, I like to quote George Young: "You talk of speed training in terms of interval quarter-miles [400 meters] and all those things. But you don't get the speed there that you get in a race."

Young spoke these words in the 1970s, when he purposely raced often. He was about to make his fourth Olympic team in his third different event. As he said, you can't match the excitement, or the effort, any other way. The racing atmosphere brings out your very best in the current race and again in those that follow.

Wonder worker that racing is, though, it must be taken as a prescription item. Underdose and you don't get the full benefit. Overdose and its harsh side effects surface. I can't prescribe one dosage for everyone. But I can leave you with these tips from a longtime user:

1. Race by the season. Run races often at certain times of year, and rebuild endurance and enthusiasm in raceless seasons.

2. Race repeatedly at shorter distances. Run 5K or less several weekends in a row, or 10K every other weekend.

3. Race below your main distance. Build speed at half that distance—5K for a 10K runner, half-marathon for a marathoner.

4. Recover well between races. Follow the time-honored rule of at least one easy day per mile of the race.

5. Don't stop racing as you prepare for a big race such as a marathon. Don't sacrifice an experience that livens up your running now and improves it later.

Date _____ *Plans* _____

Training Session

Type of run ☐ long ☐ fast ☐ easy ☐ none ☐ race

Distance _____ *Time* _____

Pace _____ per mile _____ per kilometer

Splits _____ / _____ / _____ / _____ / _____ / _____

Effort ☐ max ☐ hard ☐ moderate ☐ easy ☐ rest

Training heart rates target _____ actual _____

Warm-up _____ *Cool-down* _____ *Cross-training* _____

Training Conditions

Location _____ *Time of day* _____

People ☐ alone ☐ with group ☐ race ☐ with partner _____
                                                          name

Surface ☐ road ☐ trail ☐ track ☐ mixed _____

Terrain ☐ flat ☐ hilly ☐ mixed _____

Weather _____ *Shoes worn* _____

Diet drinks during run _____ foods during run _____

Training Rating

Success level   10   9   8   7   6   5   4   3   2   1   0

Training Comments

_____

_____

_____

You train for both the distance and speed of the marathon—with long runs at slower than race pace and short runs, faster.

LEARNING TRICKS

This week's training tips theme is upping your tempo. Semilong runs, fast runs, and short races all serve the same purpose: They acquaint you with the pace or tempo of your marathon and often ask you to run somewhat faster. While learning these tricks, check the thoughts for additional shared wisdom on the sport. Choose your program from the options listed, assign runs to the next seven days of diary pages, and add details there for completed training.

Cruiser Program

Big day: Race of 5K, or fast solo run of 1 to 3 miles (1.6 to 5K). In either case, run at least one minute per mile (35 seconds per kilometer) faster than your projected marathon pace.

Other training days: Three or four easy runs of 30 to 45 minutes each, with walking breaks optional.

Rest days: Two or three with no running, but possibly easy cross-training.

Pacer Program

Big day: Semilong run of 8 to 9 miles (13 to 15K), or half the distance of last week's long one. Run this distance nonstop at your projected marathon pace or slightly faster.

Other training days: Four or five easy runs of 30 to 60 minutes each.

Rest days: One or two with no running, but possibly easy cross-training.

Racer Program

Long day: Semilong run of 9 to 10 miles (14 to 16K), or half the distance of last week's long one. Run at your projected marathon pace or slightly faster.

Fast day: Race of 5K to 10K, or 1- to 3-mile run at current 10K race pace (1.6 to 5K; this may be broken into shorter intervals that total 1 to 3 miles—1.6 to 5K—not counting recovery periods). Warm up and cool down with easy running.

Other training days: Four easy runs of 30 to 60 minutes each.

Rest days: One with no running, but possibly easy cross-training.

Warming to the Task

Running can feel good, but not at the start. Getting into the full free flow of the run takes time.

You don't just step out the door and hit your stride in the first 100 steps. You must shift from one form of inertia (resting) to another (moving), and that transition takes more time than some runners allow.

TRAINING TIP

Build faster running into your program for several reasons: It lifts you out of a one-pace rut, adds variety to training, and gives you something challenging to do on weekends between long runs.

Running grants its physical benefits quickly—most of them in the first 20 minutes, according to some of the best minds in exercise science. Certainly we can do most of the necessary exercise running within a half-hour a day.

But running is more than an exercise. And what makes it a hobby, an athletic event, a relaxation and meditation period, a welcomed time of the day, lies in longer distances. I contend (based on no research but lots of experience) that the time beyond a half-hour is what makes running worth doing and makes us want to come back the next day for more of the same. If we stop after 20 minutes, we've stopped short of the best part. We aren't fully warmed up.

By *warm-up* we're not talking about stretching or other drills, which serve other needs besides warming up the muscles and working up a sweat. A runner warms up soonest and best by running. How much you run at that time depends on what the day holds: a long run, a fast run, or a normal run. Each has its own special warm-up requirements.

Sometimes this phase precedes the day's main run. More often it becomes a part of that run.

Date _____ *Plans* _____

Training Session

Type of run □ long □ fast □ easy □ none □ race

Distance _____ *Time* _____

Pace _____ per mile _____ per kilometer

Splits _____ / _____ / _____ / _____ / _____ / _____

Effort □ max □ hard □ moderate □ easy □ rest

Training heart rates target _____ actual _____

Warm-up _____ *Cool-down* _____ *Cross-training* _____

Training Conditions

Location _____ *Time of day* _____

People □ alone □ with group □ race □ with partner _____
name

Surface □ road □ trail □ track □ mixed _____

Terrain □ flat □ hilly □ mixed _____

Weather _____ *Shoes worn* _____

Diet drinks during run _____ foods during run _____

Training Rating

Success level   10   9   8   7   6   5   4   3   2   1   0

Training Comments

_____

_____

_____

Warm-Up Needs

Normal days: Warm slowly. In my travels I often stay in the same hotels as Kenyan runners, who in full flight are awesome to behold. Yet I see them starting their morning training runs at a shuffling pace. The Kenyans don't stay slow, of course. They work the pace up—way up—as they warm to the task.

There's no distinct borderline separating warm-up from real running. One gradually blends into the other. You may have to wait as long as a half-hour for the best running of the day to arrive.

Fast days: Start hot. Better to start a little tired than a lot tight. Think what happens on a normal day's run. You're awkward at first, your legs are stiff, your breathing is ragged.

After 5 to 10 minutes, sweating starts. Another 5 or 10 minutes later, your legs loosen and breathing settles down. You're almost ready for race pace—but only after challenging your legs and lungs at that pace with a few stride-outs of about 100 meters apiece. All these preliminaries might last 30 minutes.

Long days: Stay cool. Many a runner can't sit still before a marathon, but very few need any running warm-up before a race this long. If you train triple-figure mileage each week and plan to contend for a prize, warm up a little. If not, save your steps; you'll need them all later.

Start running—slowly—only when the gun sounds. Treat the first few miles as your warm-up time.

Warming as you go protects you against starting too fast. Better to warm up late than wear out early.

TRAINING TIP

Find a cure for "one-pace syndrome." It afflicts runners who know how to run long but have never learned to run fast. They run the same pace in races as in training, in 5Ks as in marathons.

Date _____ *Plans* _____

Training Session

Type of run □ long □ fast □ easy □ none □ race

Distance _____ *Time* _____

Pace _____ per mile _____ per kilometer

Splits _____ / _____ / _____ / _____ / _____ / _____

Effort □ max □ hard □ moderate □ easy □ rest

Training heart rates target _____ actual _____

Warm-up _____ *Cool-down* _____ *Cross-training* _____

Training Conditions

Location _____ *Time of day* _____

People □ alone □ with group □ race □ with partner _____
name

Surface □ road □ trail □ track □ mixed _____

Terrain □ flat □ hilly □ mixed _____

Weather _____ *Shoes worn* _____

Diet drinks during run _____ foods during run _____

Training Rating

Success level   10   9   8   7   6   5   4   3   2   1   0

Training Comments

_____

_____

_____

Going in Style

Stand beside a road sometime and watch a race instead of running it. You will see in the passing parade what you might not have noticed from the middle of it, focusing only on yourself and the runners within sight.

If you wouldn't have been one of the lead runners, you'll now see how wide the gap is between their pace and where yours would have put you. You'll notice also how different the front-runners look than most of those in your group.

The faster folks typically run smoother, quieter, taller, and prouder. The slower ones pound the ground harder and slump forward more and stare at their feet.

The differences in pace dictate some of the differences in appearance, but this doesn't have to be so. Slow runners may never be able to keep up with the fast runners, but they can look more like them. Faster running almost demands that they carry themselves this way. Slower pace doesn't make such demands, and bad habits can take root in these runs.

TRAINING TIP

Avoid training for maximum speed right now. But don't let it be a time for neglecting speed entirely, which can easily happen when you're piling up all that slow distance.

Slower runners naturally take shorter and lower strides, but we still can model ourselves after those who look the best. This isn't just advice about looking pretty, since running isn't a beauty contest and no style points are awarded.

It's worth mentioning because running lightly over the ground, in good head-to-toe alignment, is easier on the body than landing heavily and out of balance a thousand times every mile. It's also a little faster for the same level of effort.

Date _____ *Plans* _____

Training Session

Type of run ☐ long ☐ fast ☐ easy ☐ none ☐ race

Distance _____ **Time** _____

Pace _____ per mile _____ per kilometer

Splits _____ / _____ / _____ / _____ / _____ / _____

Effort ☐ max ☐ hard ☐ moderate ☐ easy ☐ rest

Training heart rates target _____ actual _____

Warm-up _____ **Cool-down** _____ **Cross-training** _____

Training Conditions

Location _____ **Time of day** _____

People ☐ alone ☐ with group ☐ race ☐ with partner _____
                                                              name

Surface ☐ road ☐ trail ☐ track ☐ mixed _____

Terrain ☐ flat ☐ hilly ☐ mixed _____

Weather _____ **Shoes worn** _____

Diet drinks during run _____ foods during run _____

Training Rating

Success level 10 9 8 7 6 5 4 3 2 1 0

Training Comments

_____

_____

_____

Run Softly, Run Tall

I don't claim to have picture-perfect form. But having started fast as a young runner (racing from the first week onward), I did learn habits that have stuck with me even while the runs have gone into slow motion.

TRAINING TIP

Benefit from a few fast runs. Faster training makes you a faster runner at all distances, including the marathon. A 10-second improvement per mile (6 seconds per kilometer) translates to almost 4-1/2 *minutes* for a marathoner.

If you come from a similar background of speed, remember how you looked then and try to retain it. If you've never run fast, or if your form has deteriorated, start taking corrective action. Add some faster running to your routine by way of short runs, steady or repeated, at a pace one to two minutes per mile faster than you typically go. This up-tempo running almost automatically forces you to run more efficiently.

The habits learned here transfer back to your normal running. In all runs, fastest to slowest, check your form with two tests:

1. Where do you look? The back follows the lead of the head. If you watch your feet hit the ground, you're hunched over. But if you raise your eyes to the horizon, your back naturally straightens and you come into more efficient alignment. Good running is straight-backed, tall running.

2. What do you hear? The feet announce how well you absorb shock. If you hear slap-slip-scrape-shuffle, you're hitting the ground too hard by not making full use of ankle-flex and toe-off. The less you hear at foot plant, the less likely the ground is to hurt you. Good running is springy-stepped, quiet running.

Whatever your pace, run softly and run tall. Look as though you're quietly proud of what you're doing.

Date _____ *Plans* _____

Training Session

Type of run   ☐ long   ☐ fast   ☐ easy   ☐ none   ☐ race

Distance _____   *Time* _____

Pace _____ per mile   _____ per kilometer

Splits _____ / _____ / _____ / _____ / _____ / _____

Effort   ☐ max   ☐ hard   ☐ moderate   ☐ easy   ☐ rest

Training heart rates target _____ actual _____

Warm-up _____ *Cool-down* _____ *Cross-training* _____

Training Conditions

Location _____ *Time of day* _____

People ☐ alone ☐ with group ☐ race ☐ with partner _____
                                                            name

Surface   ☐ road   ☐ trail   ☐ track   ☐ mixed _____

Terrain   ☐ flat   ☐ hilly   ☐ mixed _____

Weather _____ *Shoes worn* _____

Diet   drinks during run _____ foods during run _____

Training Rating

Success level   10   9   8   7   6   5   4   3   2   1   0

Training Comments

_____

_____

_____

Balancing Acts

Running is my job. On its best days it's a dream job, working at what otherwise would be a hobby. On its worst days it still beats any other career path I might have taken.

Even though my job revolves around writing and speaking and teaching this sport, my workdays aren't filled with running. As happens when working in a different field, I deal constantly with pressures and temptations *not* to run.

The writing, for instance, requires sitting for long stretches—the same as if the subject were, say, another hobby such as coin collecting. When I go to races, it's usually to talk about running or to cheer for other runners, not to run myself.

TRAINING TIP

Check this bonus: Added speed translates to faster racing with no apparent increase in effort. And an occasional speedy run makes marathon pace seem easier than if you'd trained only at the slower rate.

I have a wife who doesn't care to spend all of her spare time traveling to races. I have children who haven't yet left home for good and don't deserve a dad who's always out running. I have friends who don't run and don't want to talk about it.

Running has always been, and remains, a big part of my life. But each run occupies a small part of my day. I am decidedly a part-time runner. Reg Harris wrote a book by that title, *The Part-Time Runner*. Published in the mid-1980s, it disappeared too soon to tap into today's huge running market. But his title and message apply more than ever, as high-volume training programs ask us to spend more time running—while we have less of it to squeeze from our busy days.

Date _____ *Plans* _____

Training Session

Type of run ☐ long ☐ fast ☐ easy ☐ none ☐ race

Distance _____ *Time* _____

Pace _____ per mile _____ per kilometer

Splits _____ / _____ / _____ / _____ / _____ / _____

Effort ☐ max ☐ hard ☐ moderate ☐ easy ☐ rest

Training heart rates target _____ actual _____

Warm-up _____ *Cool-down* _____ *Cross-training* _____

Training Conditions

Location _____ *Time of day* _____

People ☐ alone ☐ with group ☐ race ☐ with partner _____
name

Surface ☐ road ☐ trail ☐ track ☐ mixed _____

Terrain ☐ flat ☐ hilly ☐ mixed _____

Weather _____ *Shoes worn* _____

Diet drinks during run _____ foods during run _____

Training Rating

Success level 10 9 8 7 6 5 4 3 2 1 0

Training Comments

_____

_____

_____

Finding Balance

Most of us are part-time runners. We have families, jobs, and other interests pushing our running into small corners of our day.

We aren't *given* the time to run; we must *make* it and protect it. We must also stay flexible and conservative with that time in order to keep the peace between running and our competing obligations. Adopting several rules has helped me manage this delicate balancing act:

TRAINING TIP

In your speed training, try to average at least 1 minute per mile (35 seconds per kilometer) faster than your long run and easy-day pace. If the slower running averages 8 minutes per mile (5:00 per kilometer), for instance, speed up to 7-minute miles (4:25 per kilometer) or faster.

- Schedule only one big day a week. *Big* means a long run that might train you for a marathon or a fast session that might prepare you for a short race. These days require so much extra focus and effort, if not extra time, that they're best taken infrequently and on days off from your job. A weekend day works best for most of us.

- Run no more than one race a month. Races are available in most areas much more often than that, but you risk tipping your life out of balance by entering too many of them. Factoring in travel and recovery time, a race is an all-day, or even all-weekend, commitment that can be less fun for the family than it is for you.

- Rest at least one day per week. If nothing else, the planned day off frees you from thinking you *must* find time to run every day. Make this a free-floating day of rest, available for days when your running must yield its time to other duties that can't wait until tomorrow.

Date _____ *Plans* _____

Training Session

Type of run □ long □ fast □ easy □ none □ race

Distance _____ **Time** _____

Pace _____ per mile _____ per kilometer

Splits _____ / _____ / _____ / _____ / _____ / _____

Effort □ max □ hard □ moderate □ easy □ rest

Training heart rates target _____ actual _____

Warm-up _____ **Cool-down** _____ **Cross-training** _____

Training Conditions

Location _____ **Time of day** _____

People □ alone □ with group □ race □ with partner _____
name

Surface □ road □ trail □ track □ mixed _____

Terrain □ flat □ hilly □ mixed _____

Weather _____ **Shoes worn** _____

Diet drinks during run _____ foods during run _____

Training Rating

Success level 10 9 8 7 6 5 4 3 2 1 0

Training Comments

_____

_____

_____

Rule of One

The most important rule of one on maintaining a balanced life: Average less than one hour of running a day. This doesn't mean you never go beyond an hour, but if you do go longer one day, then restore the balance by doing less in the days that follow. Averaging an hour a day keeps running in the realm of a hobby. Beyond that, it starts to seem like a second job.

Give yourself an hour on weekday workdays. Into that hour fit not only the run itself but also its surrounding activities of dressing and showering. These might leave little more than a half-hour for running.

TRAINING TIP

Save your really fast running for later—after the marathon ends and recovery from it is complete. The strength you gain now will lay the groundwork for faster racing when your emphasis shifts to speed.

Not enough, you say? I agree that a half-hour run can be absurdly easy for an experienced runner. But it also can be brutal for the best of runners. A world 10K record can be set in less than a half-hour, with time left over for a victory lap or two.

Half-hour runs can be any degree of difficulty you want to make them. In the time it takes to watch a sitcom or to eat a fast-food meal, you can gain and maintain basic aerobic fitness instead. This is enough time but not too much to run on recovery days. It's long enough to train for speed and to race well for at least a 5K.

Whatever you do in the allotted time, you always finish at the same time. You're back home or back on the job before anyone had time to miss you.

A beauty of running is that it's one of the most time-efficient sports. A runner can even train for a marathon while averaging less than an hour a day away from life's other activities.

Date _____ **Plans** _____

Training Session

Type of run   ☐ long   ☐ fast   ☐ easy   ☐ none   ☐ race

Distance _____ **Time** _____

Pace _____ per mile   _____ per kilometer

Splits _____ / _____ / _____ / _____ / _____ / _____

Effort   ☐ max   ☐ hard   ☐ moderate   ☐ easy   ☐ rest

Training heart rates   target _____   actual _____

Warm-up _____ **Cool-down** _____ **Cross-training** _____

Training Conditions

Location _____ **Time of day** _____

People   ☐ alone   ☐ with group   ☐ race   ☐ with partner _____
                                                                       name

Surface   ☐ road   ☐ trail   ☐ track   ☐ mixed _____

Terrain   ☐ flat   ☐ hilly   ☐ mixed _____

Weather _____ **Shoes worn** _____

Diet   drinks during run _____   foods during run _____

Training Rating

Success level   10   9   8   7   6   5   4   3   2   1   0

Training Comments

_____

_____

_____

_____

Once you choose a marathon, find a training course that mimics its terrain. Then take your long runs on this route.

PICKING RACES

You pass the midpoint in the training program this week. Look how far you've come—within 5 to 10 miles (8 to 16K) of the marathon distance. The long run for Cruisers averages 17 miles (28K), for Pacers 19 miles (31K), and for Racers 21 miles (34K). The race is becoming real to you, so we'll talk in this week about the menu of available marathons and about shorter races. Choose your program from the options listed, assign runs to the next seven days of diary pages, and add details there for completed training.

Cruiser Program

Big day: Long run of 16 to 18 miles (26 to 29K), or about a 2-mile (3K) increase from your last one. Mix running and walking while covering the distance no faster than your projected marathon pace.

Other training days: Three or four easy runs of 30 to 45 minutes each, with walking breaks optional.

Rest days: Two or three with no running, but possibly easy cross-training.

Pacer Program

Big day: Long run of 18 to 20 miles (29 to 32K), or about a 2-mile (3K) increase from your last one. Walking breaks optional. Run about one minute per mile (35 seconds per kilometer) slower than your projected marathon pace.

Other training days: Four or five easy runs of 30 to 60 minutes each.

Rest days: One or two with no running, but possibly easy cross-training.

Racer Program

Long day: Long run of 20 to 22 miles (32 to 35K), or about a 2-mile (3K) increase from your last one. Run about one minute per mile (35 seconds per kilometer) slower than your projected marathon pace.

Fast day: 1- to 3-mile (1.6 to 5K) run at current 10K race pace. (This may be broken into shorter intervals that total 1 to 3 miles—1.6 to 5K—not counting recovery periods.) Warm up and cool down with easy running.

Other training days: Four easy runs of 30 to 60 minutes each.

Rest days: One with no running, but possibly easy cross-training.

Pushing the Limits

Twice in two months, on the West Coast and East, I attended race directors' conferences. At both of them Topic A in the hallways and at meals, if not in the formal meetings, was what to do about the ever-slower finishers. Put another way, how long must race officials keep the course open? When can a race declare itself finished, even if all of its entrants aren't? What time limit is fair and reasonable?

These questions most concern directors of big marathons. They attract many runners (and more and more run-walkers and pure walkers) whose glory comes in finishing, no matter how long that takes.

I don't damn anyone for being slow, being ever more so myself. We wouldn't be running races now if time limits hadn't eased dramatically.

Longtime writer and longer-time runner Bob Cooper recalls how he dropped out of a 1970 marathon after seeing he wouldn't make the cutoff time. It was four hours. "Can you imagine," he asked, "the number of dreams that would be crushed if a four-hour cutoff existed in marathons today?"

I've faced even stiffer dream killers. My first marathon was Boston, and my big worry there was not finishing before the official timing ended—at 3-1/2 hours. This limit scared me into beating that deadline by 40 minutes.

Worse was the 1971 National Championship Marathon in Eugene, Oregon. An even three hours was its limit. I missed that time by a few minutes and felt a letdown akin to arriving at a party right after it ended.

TRAINING TIP

Plan to enter some 5K, 8K, or 10K races on weekends between long runs. The best place to build speed is in these short races. But don't take them so seriously that they detract from the marathon training.

Date _____ **Plans** _____

Training Session

Type of run   ☐ long   ☐ fast   ☐ easy   ☐ none   ☐ race

Distance _____ **Time** _____

Pace _____ per mile   _____ per kilometer

Splits _____ / _____ / _____ / _____ / _____ / _____

Effort   ☐ max   ☐ hard   ☐ moderate   ☐ easy   ☐ rest

Training heart rates target _____ actual _____

Warm-up _____ **Cool-down** _____ **Cross-training** _____

Training Conditions

Location _____ **Time of day** _____

People   ☐ alone   ☐ with group   ☐ race   ☐ with partner _____
                                                                                      name

Surface   ☐ road   ☐ trail   ☐ track   ☐ mixed _____

Terrain   ☐ flat   ☐ hilly   ☐ mixed _____

Weather _____ **Shoes worn** _____

Diet   drinks during run _____   foods during run _____

Training Rating

Success level   10   9   8   7   6   5   4   3   2   1   0

Training Comments

_____

_____

_____

Time Line

How times have changed. In 2002 I set a marathon PR—for the longest time announcing at a finish line. At the Yakima River Canyon Marathon the last person checked in at 8:05 and found the finish area still up and running. I didn't mind sticking around. If someone spent that long on the course, the least I could do was call her name at the end.

Yakima, with its rural road course, could be generous with its time. But runners need to know that such a liberal allotment isn't always, or even often, possible.

Races need a finish line, in time as well as distance. The question is where to draw the time line. The answer requires compromise among all the competing interests that have a say in how a race is run—and for how long.

TRAINING TIP

Limit your races to 10K during the marathon-training period. That way, you'll get the full benefit from them and still not need more than a few days to recover from the short races.

Runners, and especially late-finishing walkers, want the course to stay open at least as long as needed for them to finish on a worst-case day. They argue that their entry fee entitles them to the race's full attention for as long as needed.

Sponsors, as well as charities, ask race officials to deliver numbers. The more people who enter, the wider the exposure to a sponsor's goods and services, and the greater the charitable donations. Numbers add up the quickest at the slow end of the pack.

Volunteer helpers come out early and stay late on race day. They are the runners' hosts. They welcome almost everyone to their party, but they prefer that the guests not stay too long.

Date _____ **Plans** _____

Training Session

Type of run □ long □ fast □ easy □ none □ race

Distance _____ **Time** _____

Pace _____ per mile _____ per kilometer

Splits _____ / _____ / _____ / _____ / _____ / _____

Effort □ max □ hard □ moderate □ easy □ rest

Training heart rates target _____ actual _____

Warm-up _____ **Cool-down** _____ **Cross-training** _____

Training Conditions

Location _____ **Time of day** _____

People □ alone □ with group □ race □ with partner _____
name

Surface □ road □ trail □ track □ mixed _____

Terrain □ flat □ hilly □ mixed _____

Weather _____ **Shoes worn** _____

Diet drinks during run _____ foods during run _____

Training Rating

Success level   10   9   8   7   6   5   4   3   2   1   0

Training Comments

_____

_____

_____

Acceptable Limits

City officials and police tolerate races, often by the slimmest of margins. They dictate how long a course can stay open—or as they think of it, roads stay closed or limited to traffic. They usually have the final say on time limits, as with the 5-1/2 hours imposed on the Napa Valley Marathon by the state highway department and enforced by the California Highway Patrol.

Conflicting interests must come to consensus on when a race officially ends. As someone who has participated in marathons as a runner, sponsor, and race official (but never as a public officer), these are my views:

- Set as liberal a time limit as the politicians and police will allow and the volunteers can tolerate. State this time clearly in prerace notices, explaining exactly what will happen to people who miss the cutoff time. Will they be swept off the course, allowed to go on without traffic control, recognized or not at the finish?

- Vote with your feet. If you don't like a race's limit, don't go there. Instead support "slow-friendly" events such as the Portland Marathon. It has a designated walking division, eight hours to finish and a two-shift system of volunteers along the course.

- Run shorter races. The marathon isn't for everyone. Many of today's later finishers would be better served by the half-marathons often held along with marathons. The same time limit could apply for both distances while being doubly generous in pace for the half-marathoners.

Date _____ *Plans* _____

Training Session

Type of run □ long □ fast □ easy □ none □ race

Distance _____ **Time** _____

Pace _____ per mile _____ per kilometer

Splits _____ / _____ / _____ / _____ / _____ / _____

Effort □ max □ hard □ moderate □ easy □ rest

Training heart rates target _____ actual _____

Warm-up _____ **Cool-down** _____ **Cross-training** _____

Training Conditions

Location _____ **Time of day** _____

People □ alone □ with group □ race □ with partner _____
name

Surface □ road □ trail □ track □ mixed _____

Terrain □ flat □ hilly □ mixed _____

Weather _____ **Shoes worn** _____

Diet drinks during run _____ foods during run _____

Training Rating

Success level   10   9   8   7   6   5   4   3   2   1   0

Training Comments

_____

_____

_____

Honoring Endurance

Running a marathon is too big an effort to keep to ourselves. Individually we often dedicate our race to someone important to us, then our thoughts of that someone help keep us moving when the miles grow long.

A marathon inaugurated in 2001 took this spirit of sharing to a new high. The Oklahoma City Memorial Marathon commemorated a single event, and everyone ran to honor the same 168 people. That number died on April 19, 1995, at the time the worst terrorist act in U.S. history. Hundreds more were injured in the bombing, and uncounted thousands were scarred by it.

TRAINING TIP

Aside from the speed-training factor, running short races during marathon training supplies an element of excitement that you miss while running alone. Don't deprive yourself of this thrill for these three months.

Ground zero of that blast was the Murrah Federal Building. Now resting in its former footprint is the Oklahoma City National Memorial, which is all the more moving for its simplicity.

A reflecting pool replaced the street that once passed in front of the building. The Memorial's centerpiece is a set of 168 empty chairs. This spot was dedicated on the fifth anniversary of the tragedy. Soon afterward a pair of local runners, Thomas Hill and Chet Collier, began planning the marathon that would begin in the sixth post-tragedy April.

"From the beginning," they wrote in the race program, "our vision was to honor the dead and to join hands with the living in striving for a better, healthier, and safer future." The noblest of sentiments. But the hard, practical reality was that the organizers had less than a year to pull together a marathon and to make it a worthy tribute. They succeeded.

Date _____ **Plans** _____

Training Session

Type of run   ☐ long   ☐ fast   ☐ easy   ☐ none   ☐ race

Distance _____   **Time** _____

Pace _____ per mile   _____ per kilometer

Splits _____ / _____ / _____ / _____ / _____ / _____

Effort   ☐ max   ☐ hard   ☐ moderate   ☐ easy   ☐ rest

Training heart rates target _____   actual _____

Warm-up _____   **Cool-down** _____   **Cross-training** _____

Training Conditions

Location _____   **Time of day** _____

People   ☐ alone   ☐ with group   ☐ race   ☐ with partner _____
name

Surface   ☐ road   ☐ trail   ☐ track   ☐ mixed _____

Terrain   ☐ flat   ☐ hilly   ☐ mixed _____

Weather _____   **Shoes worn** _____

Diet drinks during run _____   foods during run _____

Training Rating

Success level   10   9   8   7   6   5   4   3   2   1   0

Training Comments

_____

_____

_____

Helping the Healing

Runners in the first Oklahoma City Memorial Marathon started at the Memorial itself, near enough to see these words etched into a wall: "We come here to remember those who were killed, those who survived and those changed forever. May all who leave here know the impact of violence. May this memorial offer comfort, strength, peace, hope and serenity."

TRAINING TIP

In place of a short race, insert a speed session. Total 1 to 3 miles (either as a straight run or as interval training) while running at about your current 10K race pace.

Oklahoma City has endured—and continues to endure—its worst nightmare. An endurance event is a fitting tribute, but the symbolic connection is imperfect.

A marathon ends within a few hours. Recovery is much slower, and never to be complete, for the families of victims.

Runner's World writer Hal Higdon, in town to speak at the marathon, visited the memorial after the race. "As my wife, Rose, and I left the museum," said Hal, "we walked past the fence where visitors leave mementos. Dozens of runners had left behind their race numbers." Hal had earlier left his own tribute.

The enduring of the April 1995 tragedy goes on in Oklahoma City. But so does the healing, in part through events like the Memorial Marathon.

Carla Naylor completed her first marathon on that Sunday in 2001. She ran it in honor of her daughter, Madison. Madison was a baby the day of the blast, housed in a nearby day care center that was badly damaged. She survived with minor injuries and, fortunately, with no memory of that day. At age six she ran across the marathon finish line holding her mother's hand.

Date _____ **Plans** _____

Training Session

Type of run   ☐ long   ☐ fast   ☐ easy   ☐ none   ☐ race

Distance _____   **Time** _____

Pace _____ per mile   _____ per kilometer

Splits _____ / _____ / _____ / _____ / _____ / _____

Effort   ☐ max   ☐ hard   ☐ moderate   ☐ easy   ☐ rest

Training heart rates target _____   actual _____

Warm-up _____   **Cool-down** _____   **Cross-training** _____

Training Conditions

Location _____   **Time of day** _____

People   ☐ alone   ☐ with group   ☐ race   ☐ with partner _____
name

Surface   ☐ road   ☐ trail   ☐ track   ☐ mixed _____

Terrain   ☐ flat   ☐ hilly   ☐ mixed _____

Weather _____   **Shoes worn** _____

Diet   drinks during run _____   foods during run _____

Training Rating

Success level   10   9   8   7   6   5   4   3   2   1   0

Training Comments

_____

_____

_____

Back to Boston

I didn't just take away from my first Boston what I'd gone there to find. I came back with something much better.

My intent in 1967 was to take care of the business of becoming a marathoner. I'd never run one before and wanted to start in the best one (this before a qualifying time was needed).

Boston wasn't a Monday race then but whenever April 19th happened to fall, which was midweek that year. I could spare only two days away from work and would spend less than 24 hours in marathon city. I didn't know anyone except my two roommates, John Clarke and Tom Murphy, and hadn't allowed time for getting to know anyone new.

Business taken care of, I flew home. The best thing I took back with me wasn't a time that would forever stand as a PR, but the list of entrants published in the *Boston Globe*. The value of that list would grow with time—as I added faces, voices, and personalities to the names.

TRAINING TIP

Consider running some of your speed training as intervals—short segments divided by walks or slow runs for recovery. A sample session is three times 1 mile (1.6K) with a five-minute break between.

The number right next to mine was assigned to a Dr. G.A. Sheehan from New Jersey. Later I saw him bylined as "George" at the top of what may have been his first published story, about Boston 1967.

That race also led to my first report to appear in *Track & Field News*. The next year we met at the Mexico City Olympics and soon afterward became a writer-editor team for *Runner's World* that stayed together the rest of his life.

In his last 25 years, everyone in running learned who George Sheehan was: the sport's best-loved writer and speaker.

Date _____ **Plans** _____

Training Session

Type of run ☐ long ☐ fast ☐ easy ☐ none ☐ race

Distance _____ **Time** _____

Pace _____ per mile _____ per kilometer

Splits _____ / _____ / _____ / _____ / _____ / _____

Effort ☐ max ☐ hard ☐ moderate ☐ easy ☐ rest

Training heart rates target _____ actual _____

Warm-up _____ **Cool-down** _____ **Cross-training** _____

Training Conditions

Location _____ **Time of day** _____

People ☐ alone ☐ with group ☐ race ☐ with partner _____
                                                                    name

Surface ☐ road ☐ trail ☐ track ☐ mixed _____

Terrain ☐ flat ☐ hilly ☐ mixed _____

Weather _____ **Shoes worn** _____

Diet drinks during run _____ foods during run _____

Training Rating

Success level 10 9 8 7 6 5 4 3 2 1 0

Training Comments

_____

_____

_____

Running Together

What strikes me most from the old Boston entry list that I've kept since 1967 is how much my friends-to-be have written about running. George Sheehan, Amby Burfoot, Ed Ayres, Tom Derderian, Hal Higdon, Ron Daws, Dave Prokop, Peter Wood, Gabe Mirkin, John J. Kelley, Kathrine Switzer, Erich Segal—writers all.

Segal wouldn't write running books but best-selling novels, starting with *Love Story*. In this and later books Segal gives minor characters the names of his runner friends, such as Walt Hewlett and Hugh Jascourt.

Names of strangers to me then, friends now, jump off that yellowed and brittle newspaper page: Bill Clark, my onetime neighbor in California . . . Orville Atkins, my roommate as we watched the Mexico City Olympics . . . the legendary John A. Kelley and Ted Corbitt . . . Flory Rodd, a not-yet-reformed smoker who ran his first marathon that day and many more with me . . . Roy Reisinger, who shared the 1996 and 2000 Olympic Track Trials with me.

TRAINING TIP

Whenever you run a short race or speed session, warm up for it with an easy run of about 10 minutes and preferably some "strides"—short runs at about the pace at which you intend to train or compete. Cool down with another easy 10 minutes or so.

I don't qualify to run Boston anymore and will never again come within an hour of the PR set there. I haven't been back to Boston on marathon weekend in more than a decade. Each year I follow this race from afar, but more closely than any other. For those few hours of the third Monday in April I don't so much remember my old time as the people who ran there with me in 1967. We've come to know each other much better now than we did that day. Times fade, friendships grow.

Date _____ *Plans* _____

Training Session

Type of run   ☐ long   ☐ fast   ☐ easy   ☐ none   ☐ race

Distance _____   *Time* _____

Pace _____ per mile   _____ per kilometer

Splits _____ / _____ / _____ / _____ / _____ / _____

Effort   ☐ max   ☐ hard   ☐ moderate   ☐ easy   ☐ rest

Training heart rates target _____   actual _____

Warm-up _____   *Cool-down* _____   *Cross-training* _____

Training Conditions

Location _____   *Time of day* _____

People   ☐ alone   ☐ with group   ☐ race   ☐ with partner _____
name

Surface   ☐ road   ☐ trail   ☐ track   ☐ mixed _____

Terrain   ☐ flat   ☐ hilly   ☐ mixed _____

Weather _____   *Shoes worn* _____

Diet   drinks during run _____   foods during run _____

Training Rating

Success level   10   9   8   7   6   5   4   3   2   1   0

Training Comments

_____

_____

_____

_____

In marathons you dress more for function than for fashion. You wear what best protects the feet and eases weather worries.

DRESSING UP

Now that you've entered the second half of the program, check yourself out as a marathoner would when the race really begins—just past the halfway point. How do you feel? Any problems with lingering pain, with chronic fatigue? How's your equipment working out? We give special attention this week to your most important equipment item: the shoes. Choose your program from the options listed, assign runs to the next seven days of diary pages, and add details there for completed training.

Cruiser Program

Big day: Semilong run of 8 to 9 miles (13 to 15K), or half the distance of last week's long one. Run this distance nonstop with no walking breaks. Run slightly faster than your projected marathon pace.

Other training days: Three or four easy runs of 30 to 45 minutes each, with walking breaks optional.

Rest days: Two or three with no running, but possibly easy cross-training.

Pacer Program

Big day: Race of 5K to 10K, or fast solo run of 1 to 3 miles (1.6 to 5K; this may be broken into intervals) at current 10K race pace. Warm up and cool down with easy running.

Other training days: Four or five easy runs of 30 to 60 minutes each.

Rest days: One or two with no running, but possibly easy cross-training.

Racer Program

Long day: Long run of 21 to 23 miles (33 to 37K), or about a 1-mile (1.6K) increase from your last one. Run about one minute per mile (35 seconds per kilometer) slower than marathon pace.

Fast day: 1- to 3-mile (1.6 to 5K) run at current 10K race pace. (This may be broken into shorter intervals that total 1 to 3 miles—1.6 to 5K—not counting recovery periods.) Warm up and cool down with easy running.

Other training days: Four easy runs of 30 to 60 minutes each.

Rest days: One with no running, but possibly easy cross-training.

On Our Feet

Bob Dolphin and his wife, Lenore, passed through my hometown on their way home from yet another of their marathons. The Dolphins, both in their 70s, travel to marathons about half the weekends of the year.

Bob runs the races; his marathon count passed 300 in 2002 and climbs by more than 20 a year. Lenore supports Bob and usually volunteers to help at the races they attend. Together they direct the Yakima River Canyon Marathon in Washington State, which was meant to be our lunchtime subject this day.

TRAINING TIP

Ask yourself, How am I adapting to the increased training? Do I feel energetic or lethargic? Am I pain-free or sore from the extra effort? Have I caught any illnesses related to the extra stress?

Shoe choices weren't on our agenda. But the subject usually comes up whenever two or more runners meet. It was guaranteed to come up this time because we were stopping by a running shop after lunch.

I noticed that Bob wore lightweight Nike shoes. The model was unfamiliar to me, but it looked like a racing shoe. "Do you run marathons in those?" I asked.

"I do," he said. "I think they are why I've run smoother and faster lately."

Such thinking runs counter to the modern gospel of shoes. We're taught that we need maximum support, and the longer we run, the more shoe we require. An industry is built around putting more into and onto our shoes, thus charging more for the end product. Bob Dolphin joins a fringe group of runners who don't buy into this concept. They think the best shoes are the least they can get by with, not the most weight their feet can lift.

Date _____ *Plans* _____

Training Session

Type of run   ☐ long   ☐ fast   ☐ easy   ☐ none   ☐ race

Distance _____   *Time* _____

Pace _____ per mile   _____ per kilometer

Splits _____ / _____ / _____ / _____ / _____ / _____

Effort   ☐ max   ☐ hard   ☐ moderate   ☐ easy   ☐ rest

Training heart rates target _____ actual _____

Warm-up _____ *Cool-down* _____ *Cross-training* _____

Training Conditions

Location _____ *Time of day* _____

People ☐ alone ☐ with group ☐ race ☐ with partner _____
                                                                    name

Surface   ☐ road   ☐ trail   ☐ track   ☐ mixed _____

Terrain   ☐ flat   ☐ hilly   ☐ mixed _____

Weather _____ *Shoes worn* _____

Diet   drinks during run _____   foods during run _____

Training Rating

Success level   10   9   8   7   6   5   4   3   2   1   0

Training Comments

_____

_____

_____

Minimal Shoes

Rich Englehart surveyed wearers of minimal shoes—and at least one rogue scientist who's convinced that less is better—for a *Marathon & Beyond* article. Rich, who thrives on running high mileage in racing shoes, sent me a list of questions because of my longtime leanings toward lighter-is-better.

"You've written a few times that you run in this type of shoe. How long has this been true?"

Forever, almost. In high school I often ran—and sometimes even raced—barefoot. And I've rarely worn socks. So my preference has always been to run as close to "naked" as possible—to feel somewhat in touch with the ground. Shoes that allow this feeling are increasingly difficult to find without going to strictly racing models that are quite expensive ounce for ounce and wear out quickly.

"Could you give a brief description of some standard characteristics of the shoes you run in?"

TRAINING TIP

Check your fatigue level. Long runs are supposed to tire you temporarily, but if the feeling lingers longer than a few days, ease the effort of your next long run by slowing the pace or taking walking breaks.

I look for the lightest possible all-purpose models, adaptable to both daily runs and races. Main requirements are plenty of flexibility in the forefoot, heels of cushy single-density material, and a "quiet" (as opposed to slapping) run.

"What typically happens if you try to run in a mainstream trainer?"

The early warning system is my Achilles tendons. The first signal that a shoe doesn't agree with me is soreness in one or both Achilles. Beyond that, I simply feel awkward in shoes that are too bulky and stiff. In general, the lighter and more flexible the shoe, the smoother the run.

Date _____ *Plans* _____

Training Session

Type of run   □ long   □ fast   □ easy   □ none   □ race

Distance _____   *Time* _____

Pace _____ per mile   _____ per kilometer

Splits _____ / _____ / _____ / _____ / _____ / _____

Effort   □ max   □ hard   □ moderate   □ easy   □ rest

Training heart rates target _____ actual _____

Warm-up _____ *Cool-down* _____ *Cross-training* _____

Training Conditions

Location _____ *Time of day* _____

People □ alone   □ with group   □ race   □ with partner _____
                                                            name

Surface   □ road   □ trail   □ track   □ mixed _____

Terrain   □ flat   □ hilly   □ mixed _____

Weather _____ *Shoes worn* _____

Diet   drinks during run _____   foods during run _____

Training Rating

Success level   10   9   8   7   6   5   4   3   2   1   0

Training Comments

_____

_____

_____

Lighten Up

More of Rich Englehart's questions and my answers on minimal shoes:

"When you mention your shoe preferences to people in the running world, what sorts of responses do you get?"

Disbelief. Like training slower to race faster or taking walk breaks to run longer, wearing lighter shoes to run injury-freer is too weird a concept for most runners to think of mimicking. They say something like, "Well, it works for you because you're a lightweight yourself and don't run many miles. But because I'm bigger and run more, I need to wear more."

I review my injury history until the listener's eyes glaze. Then I say that more of these troubles came from wearing the "right" shoes than the "wrong" ones.

TRAINING TIP

Check your pain level. Any soreness that lingers from one run to the next requires attention. It's your warning that a small problem could grow into something major if ignored.

"As onetime *Runner's World* editor you oversaw the annual shoe issue, and you once edited a magazine published by Nike. Did your contact with the shoe industry leave any lasting impressions?"

This is all ancient history. I've intentionally kept my distance from the shoe industry since the early 1980s. My impressions: Modern shoes made it possible for runners of all sizes and shapes to take to the roads and up their mileage, which made the first running boom possible. But these companies were lured into the same thinking that runners are: If some of something is good (in this case some support features), then more must be better. This isn't true with mileage or speed training, and it isn't with shoe materials—at least not for some of us.

Date _____ *Plans* _____

Training Session

Type of run   ☐ long   ☐ fast   ☐ easy   ☐ none   ☐ race

Distance _____   *Time* _____

Pace _____ per mile   _____ per kilometer

Splits _____ / _____ / _____ / _____ / _____ / _____

Effort   ☐ max   ☐ hard   ☐ moderate   ☐ easy   ☐ rest

Training heart rates   target _____   actual _____

Warm-up _____   *Cool-down* _____   *Cross-training* _____

Training Conditions

Location _____   *Time of day* _____

People   ☐ alone   ☐ with group   ☐ race   ☐ with partner _____
name

Surface   ☐ road   ☐ trail   ☐ track   ☐ mixed _____

Terrain   ☐ flat   ☐ hilly   ☐ mixed _____

Weather _____   *Shoes worn* _____

Diet   drinks during run _____   foods during run _____

Training Rating

Success level   10   9   8   7   6   5   4   3   2   1   0

Training Comments

_____

_____

_____

══ Watch It ══

Return with me now to the not-too-distant past when watches still had hands. Timing our runs was an inexact act as recently as the 1970s. Back then we would set the watch's hour and minute hands to 12, wait for the second hand to reach the top, then start running. Later we would grab a finish time within a minute or so from accurate.

Sometimes a passer-by would ask, "Can you tell me what time it is?" We'd shrug, leaving the asker to wonder why anyone would wear a watch but not know what time it was.

TRAINING TIP

Rule for running with minor aches and pains: If they cause you to limp or if pain increases as you run, stop. But if form is normal and pain eases as you warm up, continue cautiously.

Only once in that era did my race time come close to matching the time of day. That happened at the Boston Marathon, which began at noon. Even there, timing was an estimate. Did the hands read 2:48-something, 2:49-plus, or 2:50-or-so? I waited hours for the official verdict.

Our old wristwatches weren't just inexact; they were unreliable. "Waterproof" didn't mean sweatproof. The stem gummed up with salt until it froze, leaving the watch to die from no rewinding.

Leaping across the decades, we now wear five-function digital watches while running—and still fumble and shrug when asked the time of day. This hasn't changed, but almost everything else in time-keeping has.

The digital wrist-stopwatch was one of running's greatest inventions. It gave runners instant and precise race results. These watches created the PR—the precious personal record—by tuning us in to our own times.

Date _____ *Plans* _____

Training Session

Type of run ☐ long ☐ fast ☐ easy ☐ none ☐ race

Distance _____ *Time* _____

Pace _____ per mile _____ per kilometer

Splits _____ / _____ / _____ / _____ / _____ / _____

Effort ☐ max ☐ hard ☐ moderate ☐ easy ☐ rest

Training heart rates target _____ actual _____

Warm-up _____ *Cool-down* _____ *Cross-training* _____

Training Conditions

Location _____ *Time of day* _____

People ☐ alone ☐ with group ☐ race ☐ with partner _____
_{name}

Surface ☐ road ☐ trail ☐ track ☐ mixed _____

Terrain ☐ flat ☐ hilly ☐ mixed _____

Weather _____ *Shoes worn* _____

Diet drinks during run _____ foods during run _____

Training Rating

Success level 10 9 8 7 6 5 4 3 2 1 0

Training Comments

_____

_____

_____

=== **Managing Time** ===

With progress can come problems. Modern watches can make time too important by splitting it too finely and in too many ways.

Time can put so much pressure on runners that they escape by going watchless, thereby missing the good a watch can give them. Here are four ways I've made friends with the watch to keep time from running me:

1. Limit the risky combination of known time and known distance to races and a very few extra-special training runs. Knowing exactly how far *and* how fast you go tempts you to turn even the easier days into races against time. Either run the distance without timing yourself most days, or run for a time period without checking the distance.

2. Turn the watch on at the first running step, off at the last. Don't touch it and seldom look at it in between. This extends to checking splits on daily runs, when thinking you're too fast or too slow could spoil an otherwise just-right effort. Let whatever happens happen between punching in and punching out.

3. Run silently. Today's watches can be programmed to beep at selected intervals. Keep them quiet. Listen to voices inside, not to signals from your wrist.

4. Start over every day. Keep the latest run's time on your watch until the next one starts. Zeroing the watch at that time is a vital and visible reminder that yesterday's run is done and gone, and you're only as good as what you do today.

TRAINING TIP

If you're hurting slightly, use the first 10 minutes of the run as your test. Decide only after this warm-up whether to complete the day's run. Sometimes stopping does you more good than continuing.

Date _____ **Plans** _____

Training Session

Type of run   ☐ long   ☐ fast   ☐ easy   ☐ none   ☐ race

Distance _____   **Time** _____

Pace _____ per mile   _____ per kilometer

Splits _____ / _____ / _____ / _____ / _____ / _____

Effort   ☐ max   ☐ hard   ☐ moderate   ☐ easy   ☐ rest

Training heart rates   target _____   actual _____

Warm-up _____   **Cool-down** _____   **Cross-training** _____

Training Conditions

Location _____   **Time of day** _____

People   ☐ alone   ☐ with group   ☐ race   ☐ with partner _____
name

Surface   ☐ road   ☐ trail   ☐ track   ☐ mixed _____

Terrain   ☐ flat   ☐ hilly   ☐ mixed _____

Weather _____   **Shoes worn** _____

Diet   drinks during run _____   foods during run _____

Training Rating

Success level   10   9   8   7   6   5   4   3   2   1   0

Training Comments

_____

_____

_____

What to Wear Where

The San Diego Marathon handed me a T-shirt I'll never wear. It's a perfectly fine shirt—nice colors and fabric, good fit—from a fine event. But the shirt carries the label "Finisher," which I wasn't. The unwritten laws of T-shirt wear proclaim, "Thou shalt not pretend to be what you're not." Neither is it allowed to tape over the offending word, or write "Non" in front of it, or circle it in red and draw a diagonal line through "Finisher."

No, I'll never be able to wear that San Diego Marathon shirt. But I'll keep it, unused, as a reminder that this type of shirt must be earned.

I'm asked by people who know how often I travel to races, "How many T-shirts do you have?" They think the count must be in the hundreds. If I had kept them all, we'd have to add a room to our house or rent a storage unit to hold them.

TRAINING TIP

During times of minor injury, substitute another activity for the scheduled run. Bicycling, swimming, running in water, or walking seldom aggravate the problem but still give decent training effects.

But I'm not much of a saver. With a few exceptions I keep only the shirts worn regularly, and then only until they start showing their age. These never number more than 10 and never overflow a single drawer. The rejects go to Goodwill. If you come to my hometown and see a homeless person wearing the shirt of some faraway 10K, you can guess at the source.

The other "keepers" are marathon "Finisher" shirts. And I wear them only on special, usually public, occasions. This prolongs their life and my memories of what it took to earn them.

Date _____ Plans _____

Training Session

Type of run □ long □ fast □ easy □ none □ race

Distance _____ **Time** _____

Pace _____ per mile _____ per kilometer

Splits _____ / _____ / _____ / _____ / _____ / _____

Effort □ max □ hard □ moderate □ easy □ rest

Training heart rates target _____ actual _____

Warm-up _____ **Cool-down** _____ **Cross-training** _____

Training Conditions

Location _____ **Time of day** _____

People □ alone □ with group □ race □ with partner _____

name

Surface □ road □ trail □ track □ mixed _____

Terrain □ flat □ hilly □ mixed _____

Weather _____ **Shoes worn** _____

Diet drinks during run _____ foods during run _____

Training Rating

Success level 10 9 8 7 6 5 4 3 2 1 0

Training Comments

_____

_____

_____

Carrying Messages

Not just any shirt will do in a marathon. It can't, of course, be from the current race even if the shirt doesn't say "Finisher."

I see a few runners wearing the shirt from that day's marathon. They have to be newcomers who haven't yet learned that the code of the road deems this practice uncool.

My shirt has to make some kind of statement. But it isn't the one I saw a few times in a recent marathon. These are the tough-talking statements that some shirt makers favor. One read, "Four runners, three trophies. Done your speedwork?"

For most of us, running a marathon isn't about beating anyone, winning any prize, or maybe even about speed. It's about dealing with the distance as best we can, where the only competition is with ourselves.

TRAINING TIP

Treat illnesses with the greatest respect. *Never* run with a fever, and *always* rest a cold during its heaviest phase. Failure to take a few days off can penalize you for several weeks—and blow the whole program.

So the best T-shirt statement doesn't express bravado. Instead it recognizes the need for all the help we can get and all the sharing we can do.

In every marathon I see dedications to a parent, a spouse, a child, or a friend. I've worn one honoring George Sheehan. I've worn another, in the Portland Marathon, that showed solidarity with the training group I'd spoken to before the race. A growing number of shirts announce support for Team in Training, the leukemia fund-raiser.

My current statement isn't that dramatic or obvious. I simply wear the shirt from the last completed marathon, hoping that what earned it will be there to spend again this time.

Date _____ *Plans* _____

Training Session

Type of run □ long □ fast □ easy □ none □ race

Distance _____ *Time* _____

Pace _____ per mile _____ per kilometer

Splits _____ / _____ / _____ / _____ / _____ / _____

Effort □ max □ hard □ moderate □ easy □ rest

Training heart rates target _____ actual _____

Warm-up _____ *Cool-down* _____ *Cross-training* _____

Training Conditions

Location _____ *Time of day* _____

People □ alone □ with group □ race □ with partner _____
                                                              name

Surface □ road □ trail □ track □ mixed _____

Terrain □ flat □ hilly □ mixed _____

Weather _____ *Shoes worn* _____

Diet drinks during run _____ foods during run _____

Training Rating

Success level 10 9 8 7 6 5 4 3 2 1 0

Training Comments

_____

_____

_____

Train in whatever weather greets you on that day. This prepares you for the one factor you can't control on raceday.

WEATHERING STORMS

One month to marathon day! Besides planning your training between now and then, plan your travel. How will you get to the race site, and with whom? When will you arrive there? Where will you stay? Plan also how you'll deal with the weather, which you can't control but can accommodate. Choose your program from the options listed, assign runs to the next seven days of diary pages, and add details there for completed training.

Cruiser Program

Big day: Race of 5K, or fast solo run of 1 to 3 miles (1.6 to 5K). In either case, run at least one minute per mile (35 seconds per kilometer) faster than your projected marathon pace.

Other training days: Three or four easy runs of 30 to 45 minutes each, with walking breaks optional.

Rest days: Two or three with no running, but possibly easy cross-training.

Pacer Program

Big day: Semilong run of 9 to 10 miles (15 to 16K), or half the distance of your last long one. Run this distance nonstop at your projected marathon pace or slightly faster.

Other training days: Four or five easy runs of 30 to 60 minutes each.

Rest days: One or two with no running, but possibly easy cross-training.

Racer Program

Long day: Semilong run of 10 to 11 miles (16 to 18K), or approximately half the distance of last week's long one. Run at your projected marathon pace or slightly faster.

Fast day: Race of 5K to 10K, or 1- to 3-mile (1.6 to 5K) run at current 10K race pace. (This may be broken into shorter intervals that total 1 to 3 miles—1.6 to 5K—not counting recovery periods.) Warm up and cool down with easy running.

Other training days: Four easy runs of 30 to 60 minutes each.

Rest days: One with no running, but possibly easy cross-training.

Hot Date

John McGee is an idea man whose running ideas usually succeed. He headed a committee that revived the Edmonton Marathon in Alberta after an earlier race in that city had died in 1994, and the new race has grown to 10 times the old one's size. Later, John joined the successful effort to bring the World Championships to this Canadian city (and he directed the marathons there in 2001).

An idea man takes risks. One of his riskiest moves as chairman of the Edmonton Marathon was to make it an evening race. "We were looking for something to set us apart," said John. "No other marathon in North America starts at that hour."

This also meant that no other marathon runs a greater risk of hot weather. It would start in the heat of the day, and nearly everyone would finish before dark. The race gambled on a cool evening, and lost. The temperature would exceed 80 degrees Fahrenheit (30 degrees Celsius).

TRAINING TIP

Select a marathon where weather is likely to be favorable. The kindest days for a marathoner feature temperatures around 50 degrees Fahrenheit (10 degrees Celsius), with calm winds and cloudy skies.

At packet pickup that day the question on every runner's mind and lips was some variation of "How do I handle the heat?" I heard it answered first by marathon authority Jeff Galloway, who spoke gently but honestly: "This isn't a day to be thinking about PRs. Start very slowly, listen to your body, and save the faster race for your next one."

Groping for a positive message, I told runners that this race would be a different kind of experience but not necessarily a bad one. Each one, even a hot one, has something to teach.

Date _____ **Plans** _____

Training Session

Type of run ☐ long   ☐ fast   ☐ easy   ☐ none   ☐ race

Distance _____   **Time** _____

Pace _____ per mile   _____ per kilometer

Splits _____ / _____ / _____ / _____ / _____ / _____

Effort   ☐ max   ☐ hard   ☐ moderate   ☐ easy   ☐ rest

Training heart rates target _____ actual _____

Warm-up _____ **Cool-down** _____ **Cross-training** _____

Training Conditions

Location _____ **Time of day** _____

People ☐ alone   ☐ with group   ☐ race   ☐ with partner _____
                                                                    name

Surface   ☐ road   ☐ trail   ☐ track   ☐ mixed _____

Terrain   ☐ flat   ☐ hilly   ☐ mixed _____

Weather _____ **Shoes worn** _____

Diet   drinks during run _____   foods during run _____

Training Rating

Success level   10   9   8   7   6   5   4   3   2   1   0

Training Comments

_____

_____

_____

131

Not So Hot

A "bad" day for running can still leave behind good memories. One such for me was the notorious "Run for the Hoses" Boston. Faced with a starting-line temperature of 97 degrees Fahrenheit (37 degrees Celsius), runners threw away their pacing plans and time goals. They started cautiously, listened to how they felt, stayed safe, and tried to finish upright. Medical problems were surprisingly few that day.

That was my slowest marathon to date. But for a poor hot-weather runner who hadn't trained at all for those conditions, I felt surprisingly good all the way.

TRAINING TIP

You can't pick a perfect marathon day but must take whatever weather comes that day. Prepare for whatever it might bring by training long or fast as scheduled, regardless of the day's conditions.

All these years later, that day in Boston remains one of my most memorable marathons. The lesson from that marathon: You don't pick your race-day conditions; they pick you. You don't welcome the heat, but you can take more of it than you'd imagined.

I was tempted to say that the organizers for the 2002 Edmonton Marathon made a mistake by scheduling a summertime marathon at five o'clock in the afternoon. I might have suggested a shorter race—say, a "10 at 10" of 10K at 10 P.M.—on a solstice evening that stayed light that long in the far north, then a marathon at its traditional early-morning hour.

Now I see that the evening start wasn't a bad idea. Edmonton wanted to give runners a different experience, and the experiment didn't fail.

About 1,900 people finished the marathon and the half. Those having problems (other than slower-than-hoped-for times) were fewer than feared. Oh, the stories they'll all tell in years to come!

Date _____ *Plans* _____

Training Session

Type of run ☐ long ☐ fast ☐ easy ☐ none ☐ race

Distance _____ *Time* _____

Pace _____ per mile _____ per kilometer

Splits _____ / _____ / _____ / _____ / _____ / _____

Effort ☐ max ☐ hard ☐ moderate ☐ easy ☐ rest

Training heart rates target _____ actual _____

Warm-up _____ *Cool-down* _____ *Cross-training* _____

Training Conditions

Location _____ *Time of day* _____

People ☐ alone ☐ with group ☐ race ☐ with partner _____
                                                                name

Surface ☐ road ☐ trail ☐ track ☐ mixed _____

Terrain ☐ flat ☐ hilly ☐ mixed _____

Weather _____ *Shoes worn* _____

Diet drinks during run _____ foods during run _____

Training Rating

Success level 10 9 8 7 6 5 4 3 2 1 0

Training Comments

_____

_____

_____

Winter Wanderland

Winter in the United States isn't a single condition but many seasons all at once. We have a vast range of temperatures as well as distance between Alaska at the Northwest and Florida in the Southeast, with every shade of difference in between.

How U.S. runners deal with winters depends on where we live. Winter in Minnesota means brutal cold and heavy snow. Winter in my home state of Oregon means persistent rain. Winter in Hawaii means . . . well, the same perfection as the rest of the year.

TRAINING TIP

View the bad-weather training days as opportunities rather than penalties. They give you the chance to test your clothing, shoes, pacing, and toughness under the most trying conditions.

Runners in the far North bundle up and often find that cross-country skiing better suits the season than their usual run. Runners in the wet Northwest train in waterproof jackets, hats, and wet shoes. Runners everywhere that's cold look with envy on those in the sunbelt who can go out in mid-February while wearing only shorts and a short-sleeved shirt.

Today nearly every cold-climate marathoner runs through the winter. Improvements in clothing—fabrics that are both light and weatherproof—have enhanced runners' comfort levels. In fact, many runners now admit that training in the cold of winter is easier on them physically than the same running in the heat of summer. You can always add another layer against the cold, but you can only strip down so far in the heat.

It is no accident that the American state traditionally producing the most top runners per capita is also one of the coldest: Minnesota. Think of them as you dash through the snow.

Date _____ *Plans* _____

Training Session

Type of run □ long □ fast □ easy □ none □ race

Distance _____ *Time* _____

Pace _____ per mile _____ per kilometer

Splits _____ / _____ / _____ / _____ / _____ / _____

Effort □ max □ hard □ moderate □ easy □ rest

Training heart rates target _____ actual _____

Warm-up _____ *Cool-down* _____ *Cross-training* _____

Training Conditions

Location _____ *Time of day* _____

People □ alone □ with group □ race □ with partner _____
name

Surface □ road □ trail □ track □ mixed _____

Terrain □ flat □ hilly □ mixed _____

Weather _____ *Shoes worn* _____

Diet drinks during run _____ foods during run _____

Training Rating

Success level 10 9 8 7 6 5 4 3 2 1 0

Training Comments

_____

_____

_____

Out in the Cold

Now if Richard Leutzinger had asked about running through the Oregon winter, I could have answered him with some authority. I'm into my third decade of this wet and gray (but rarely cold or snowy) season here.

But Richard already knew about this state. He had lived in Eugene once and would again after retirement. Our winters wouldn't shock him, but he knew none besides those on the West Coast.

Richard wrote, "I thought about you while reading the story about the NCAA Cross-Country Championships." The meet was run in Ames, Iowa, where the wind chilled the temperature far below zero.

"The Iowa winters didn't have any influence on you to move west, did they?" asked Richard. "I'd be interested to read something about running in extreme cold weather, which I've never done.

"Are the risks from falling on the ice, or breathing in the cold? How do runners dress? Do people in cold climates run on StairMasters instead of going outdoors and 'really running'?"

He'd have to ask those questions of my friends who stayed in Iowa, or those to the north in Minnesota, or in upstate New York or Edmonton. Real winter running is a distant memory to me now.

Since leaving the Midwest, I've never missed running in true winter, but I've missed true summer even less. You can warm up on all but the coldest days but can't cool down on the hot, humid ones. Frozen feels better than fried.

TRAINING TIP

Assume that the apparent temperature will jump by 20 degrees Fahrenheit (10 degrees Celsius) when you start to run. A 20-degree Fahrenheit (−5 Celsius) day will warm up to feel like a tolerable 40 degrees Fahrenheit (5 Celsius).

Date _____ *Plans* _____

Training Session

Type of run □ long □ fast □ easy □ none □ race

Distance _____ **Time** _____

Pace _____ per mile _____ per kilometer

Splits _____ / _____ / _____ / _____ / _____ / _____

Effort □ max □ hard □ moderate □ easy □ rest

Training heart rates target _____ actual _____

Warm-up _____ **Cool-down** _____ **Cross-training** _____

Training Conditions

Location _____ **Time of day** _____

People □ alone □ with group □ race □ with partner _____
                                                                    name

Surface □ road □ trail □ track □ mixed _____

Terrain □ flat □ hilly □ mixed _____

Weather _____ **Shoes worn** _____

Diet drinks during run _____ foods during run _____

Training Rating

Success level   10   9   8   7   6   5   4   3   2   1   0

Training Comments

_____

_____

_____

Weathering Winter

A sampling of comments on the cold from runners who go out in it all winter:

John McGee from Alberta: "I put six small hex-head sheet-metal screws in the sole of each shoe. They provide me with great traction on both snow and ice, and entertain the neighborhood with their sound and sparks."

Cathy Troisi from upstate New York: "If ice is visible, the run is doable. It's the 'black ice' that's the problem, especially being out before sunrise. I have fallen a couple of times while running in winter (one slight concussion, the other times were just butt bruises). But StairMaster is not in my vocabulary. I still need to go outside daily."

Richard Watson from Missouri: "When I run with the temperature well below freezing, I put a very heavy wool mitten in a strategic place in my shorts, and that does the trick. Not that (God forbid) at my age I want to be a father."

TRAINING TIP

On cold and windy days, run the worst part first. On an out-and-back course, run the "out" portion into the wind. You'll instantly feel better after turning around and starting back with a tailwind.

Michael Musca from Maine: "Clothing technology has made outdoor activity almost pleasurable. For instance, I often run in near-zero windy conditions in relative comfort. And other nut cases choose to run with me at 5 A.M."

Bob Abbott from Minnesota: "When the paths are icy and snow-packed, it does force you to slow down somewhat, but that gives the body time to recuperate. Many runners here cross-train during the winter months, running on snowshoes. Others cross-country ski. Anyone who hibernates misses getting out in the winter wonderland and enjoying what the season has to offer."

Date _____ **Plans** _____

Training Session

Type of run ☐ long ☐ fast ☐ easy ☐ none ☐ race

Distance _____ **Time** _____

Pace _____ per mile _____ per kilometer

Splits _____ / _____ / _____ / _____ / _____ / _____

Effort ☐ max ☐ hard ☐ moderate ☐ easy ☐ rest

Training heart rates target _____ actual _____

Warm-up _____ **Cool-down** _____ **Cross-training** _____

Training Conditions

Location _____ **Time of day** _____

People ☐ alone ☐ with group ☐ race ☐ with partner _____
                                                                        name

Surface ☐ road ☐ trail ☐ track ☐ mixed _____

Terrain ☐ flat ☐ hilly ☐ mixed _____

Weather _____ **Shoes worn** _____

Diet drinks during run _____ foods during run _____

Training Rating

Success level 10 9 8 7 6 5 4 3 2 1 0

Training Comments

_____

_____

_____

Into the Wind

Standing at the 23-mile (37K) mark of the Napa Valley Marathon, watching the runners pass by, I heard one of them spit out the "S" word, then, "Here we go again."

A bend in the course had given him a break from the headwind, but now he faced it again. He put his head down and leaned into it because the day gave him no choice.

Napa's race seemed bedeviled that year, and I'm sorry for that. It's one of my best trips each March and one of my top five favorite places to run. Napa Valley had lost its title sponsor, and the host hotel was undergoing a major remodeling that cut back the expo and prerace dinner. Runners took little notice of all this as they obsessed about the weather. Will it rain? And if it does, what should I wear?

The speakers made light of the prospect. "You can blame me," I said at dinner. "I brought this with me from Oregon, where if we don't run in the winter rain we hardly run at all."

Rich Benyo, a co-director of the race, said, "Whatever happens, the race will go on. Marathons aren't canceled for anything less than a world war."

Dick Beardsley, holder of Napa's course record, said conditions are relative. "This is one factor in running that you can't control. You have to take the days as they come."

TRAINING TIP

On the hottest days, figure the "20-degree rule" (10 degrees Celsius) will work against you. A comfortably warm temperature will soon feel quite hot, so dress and pace yourself for the higher reading.

Dick knows. His life course has taken him from sensational to terrible, and he now takes all his days one by one. He had blown in the winds of misfortune for years at a time. He could deal with this headwind for a few hours.

Date _____ **Plans** _____

Training Session

Type of run   □ long   □ fast   □ easy   □ none   □ race

Distance _____   **Time** _____

Pace _____ per mile   _____ per kilometer

Splits _____ / _____ / _____ / _____ / _____ / _____

Effort   □ max   □ hard   □ moderate   □ easy   □ rest

Training heart rates target _____ actual _____

Warm-up _____ **Cool-down** _____ **Cross-training** _____

Training Conditions

Location _____ **Time of day** _____

People   □ alone   □ with group   □ race   □ with partner _____
                                                                    name

Surface   □ road   □ trail   □ track   □ mixed _____

Terrain   □ flat   □ hilly   □ mixed _____

Weather _____ **Shoes worn** _____

Diet   drinks during run _____   foods during run _____

Training Rating

Success level   10   9   8   7   6   5   4   3   2   1   0

Training Comments

_____

_____

_____

Staying the Course

As the featured speaker at a wet and windy Napa Valley Marathon, Dick Beardsley wowed the crowd. First we laughed at his humble beginnings in running and the marathon, then we cheered his sub-2:10 and sub-2:09 marathons, then we hurt for him as he suffered accidents that drove him into prescription-drug problems, then finally we celebrated his recovery.

Dick has written a book titled *Staying the Course*. And that's what he urged these runners to do.

I didn't even step onto the course as a runner that year. But watching others run wasn't a bad substitute for running myself. I didn't know many of these runners by name or face, but I knew them all by what they had to do to get to and through this race. I not only cheered for them but also felt for them, especially this day. It turned into one of the worst marathon days I've ever seen.

Rain turned heavy, with hail at times, and a high wind sucked away body heat along with enthusiasm. A point-to-point course like Napa's can giveth when the wind is right, but it tooketh away this time as an almost constant headwind.

TRAINING TIP

Quit complaining about the weather. The wind won't die, rain won't stop, and temperature won't shift as a favor to you. Adapt your training to the conditions and take pride in accepting them on their terms.

Standing at 23 miles (37K), this was one of the few times I've ever pitied the passing runners instead of envying them. But I admired even more than ever those who'd come this far and would stay the course in the face of these conditions. Doing this would serve them well on better days to come.

Date _____ **Plans** _____

Training Session

Type of run   ☐ long   ☐ fast   ☐ easy   ☐ none   ☐ race

Distance _____   **Time** _____

Pace _____ per mile   _____ per kilometer

Splits _____ / _____ / _____ / _____ / _____ / _____

Effort   ☐ max   ☐ hard   ☐ moderate   ☐ easy   ☐ rest

Training heart rates target _____ actual _____

Warm-up _____ **Cool-down** _____ **Cross-training** _____

Training Conditions

Location _____ **Time of day** _____

People ☐ alone   ☐ with group   ☐ race   ☐ with partner _____
name

Surface   ☐ road   ☐ trail   ☐ track   ☐ mixed _____

Terrain   ☐ flat   ☐ hilly   ☐ mixed _____

Weather _____ **Shoes worn** _____

Diet   drinks during run _____   foods during run _____

Training Rating

Success level   10   9   8   7   6   5   4   3   2   1   0

Training Comments

_____

_____

_____

Marathoners hit two peaks. One is on raceday, of course. The other comes weeks earlier, in your longest training run.

WEEK 10

PEAKING OUT

All programs peak this week, with the longest run of this training period. Distances reach at least 18 miles (29K), or about two-thirds of a marathon. But it's strongly recommended that first-time marathoners train at least 20 miles (32K) once. This is a major mental hurdle, and once cleared it gives the confidence needed to cover the remaining distance on race day. Choose your program from the options listed, assign runs to the next seven days of diary pages, and add details there for completed training.

Cruiser Program

Big day: Long run of 18 to 20 miles (29 to 32K), or about a 2-mile (3K) increase from your last one. Mix running and walking while covering the distance no faster than your projected marathon pace.

Other training days: Three or four easy runs of 30 to 45 minutes each, with walking breaks optional.

Rest days: Two or three with no running, but possibly easy cross-training.

Pacer Program

Big day: Long run of 20 to 22 miles (32 to 35K), or about a 2-mile (3K) increase from your last one. Walking breaks optional. Run about one minute per mile (35 seconds per kilometer) slower than your projected marathon pace.

Other training days: Four or five easy runs of 30 to 60 minutes each.

Rest days: One or two with no running, but possibly easy cross-training.

Racer Program

Long day: Long run of 22 to 24 miles (35 to 38K), or about a 1-mile (1.6K) increase from your last one. Run about one minute per mile (35 seconds per kilometer) slower than marathon pace.

Fast day: 1- to 3-mile (1.6 to 5K) run at current 10K race pace. (This may be broken into shorter intervals that total 1 to 3 miles—1.6 to 5K—not counting recovery periods.) Warm up and cool down with easy running.

Other training days: Four easy runs of 30 to 60 minutes each.

Rest days: One with no running, but possibly easy cross-training.

Aiming to Please

Goals have never been good to me. At least not the types of goal setting that athletes are asked to do: Aim for the stars; your reach must exceed your grasp; if you don't dream it, you can't do it.

I caved in to the pressure of such goals from the start. In my first high school mile I aimed to beat the big boys. The only one beaten up by a too-fast start and quitting the race after little more than a lap was me.

TRAINING TIP

Prepare for the most important run of this program: your longest (and in fact final long one). It most closely resembles the marathon itself, and you run it three weeks before race day.

"Goals are stopping places," I once wrote. Either you reach them and stop because you're satisfied, or you don't reach them and stop out of frustration. By setting high goals, you set yourself up for high pressure and a high probability of failure. Low goals lead to low pressure and surprising results.

My goals are never lower than on normal daily runs. The aim there is to run 10 minutes and then decide what more to do—if anything. This minimum standard gets me out the door without having to face an imposing assignment for the day. Once moving, I almost always go well past the minimum.

"At-least" goals act as floors, not ceilings. They give you a solid platform to spring from rather than an elusive target to bat at. Instead of reaching for the highest point you might touch, you see how far you can exceed a minimum standard. Instead of straining to make things happen, you relax and let them happen.

Reduce the chances of disappointing yourself by lowering too-high goals. Increase the chances of surprising yourself by setting at-least goals.

Date _____ **Plans** _____

Training Session

Type of run □ long □ fast □ easy □ none □ race

Distance _____ **Time** _____

Pace _____ per mile _____ per kilometer

Splits _____ / _____ / _____ / _____ / _____ / _____

Effort □ max □ hard □ moderate □ easy □ rest

Training heart rates target _____ actual _____

Warm-up _____ **Cool-down** _____ **Cross-training** _____

Training Conditions

Location _____ **Time of day** _____

People □ alone □ with group □ race □ with partner _____
                                                                name

Surface □ road □ trail □ track □ mixed _____

Terrain □ flat □ hilly □ mixed _____

Weather _____ **Shoes worn** _____

Diet drinks during run _____ foods during run _____

Training Rating

Success level   10   9   8   7   6   5   4   3   2   1   0

Training Comments

_____

_____

_____

Exceeding Expectations

A tale of two marathons: They seem to have little in common except their distance. They were spaced 33 years apart, one on the East Coast and the other one the West, my fastest and next-to-slowest.

Race one: Boston 1967 was my marathon debut, and running it at the pace of my longest training run seemed a reasonable goal. I started as planned but steadily nudged up the pace. To my shocked delight I averaged 1-1/2 minutes per mile (about 1 minute per kilometer) faster than I'd hoped.

TRAINING TIP

Give yourself a minitaper before the longest run. Rest up for it by keeping the last few runs quite easy and possibly substituting a day of rest for one of the easier runs.

Race two: Decades later my aims were nil. I'd entered but almost not started the Napa Valley Marathon after a minor injury had limited training. The excitement of race day drew me to the start line, though even then the plan was to go no more than half a marathon before hailing a sag-wagon.

The early see-how-I-feel period passed while giving no compelling reason to stop. The half-marathon came and went with a promise to a companion, *Marathon & Beyond* publisher Jan Seeley, to go 16 miles (26K) with her. She stopped as planned. I said I'd like to run "a couple more miles"—which led to even more, until I'd sauntered across the finish line.

I'm not quite ready to tell you, "Aim low," which sounds like a pathway to mediocrity. What I do suggest is taking a look at goals from another direction. Instead of thinking of them as the most you might achieve, consider them as the least you're willing to accept.

Meeting expectations is rewarding. Beating them is even better.

Date _____ *Plans* _____

Training Session

Type of run   □ long   □ fast   □ easy   □ none   □ race

Distance _____   **Time** _____

Pace _____ per mile   _____ per kilometer

Splits _____ / _____ / _____ / _____ / _____ / _____

Effort   □ max   □ hard   □ moderate   □ easy   □ rest

Training heart rates target _____ actual _____

Warm-up _____ **Cool-down** _____ **Cross-training** _____

Training Conditions

Location _____ **Time of day** _____

People □ alone   □ with group   □ race   □ with partner _____
                                                                    name

Surface   □ road   □ trail   □ track   □ mixed _____

Terrain   □ flat   □ hilly   □ mixed _____

Weather _____ **Shoes worn** _____

Diet   drinks during run _____   foods during run _____

Training Rating

Success level   10   9   8   7   6   5   4   3   2   1   0

Training Comments

_____

_____

_____

Olympic Ambitions

Here is the tale of a runner who shows that a practice I propose, setting low goals, isn't as weird as it might seem. The woman involved, Christine Clark, MD, is anything but an underachiever, athletically or professionally.

Many American marathoners aimed higher in the year 2000 than Dr. Clark. None achieved more on the biggest international stage.

When first spotted during U.S. television coverage from the Olympic Games in Sydney, Chris lagged near the back. She might have appeared to be overwhelmed by the occasion. But no, Chris was simply running her own pace while many women ahead of her were running too fast for their talents. She calmly worked her way up into the top 20 finishers. And in the process she set a personal best on a windy day and hilly course that yielded few such times.

She was as surprised as anyone that she had even reached the Sydney Games. Winning the U.S. Women's Marathon Trials hadn't figured into her prerace plans there. She hadn't aimed low in the race at Columbia, South Carolina, but had realistically said she hoped to break into the top 20.

TRAINING TIP

Make sure you get your drinks during the longest training run. Scout the course in advance for drink stops. If you don't find enough of them, stash bottles of your favorite fluid along the route.

Before the race she had told a reporter from her hometown of Anchorage, "If you train really hard, you're going to have a good day. And sometimes, for no reason you can account for, you have a great day."

You can't will such days to happen. You do the training, then take your chances on what kind of race day it will be.

Date _____ *Plans* _____

Training Session

Type of run   □ long   □ fast   □ easy   □ none   □ race

Distance _____ *Time* _____

Pace _____ per mile   _____ per kilometer

Splits _____ / _____ / _____ / _____ / _____ / _____

Effort   □ max   □ hard   □ moderate   □ easy   □ rest

Training heart rates target _____ actual _____

Warm-up _____ *Cool-down* _____ *Cross-training* _____

Training Conditions

Location _____ *Time of day* _____

People □ alone □ with group □ race □ with partner _____

name

Surface   □ road   □ trail   □ track   □ mixed _____

Terrain   □ flat   □ hilly   □ mixed _____

Weather _____ *Shoes worn* _____

Diet drinks during run _____ foods during run _____

Training Rating

Success level   10   9   8   7   6   5   4   3   2   1   0

Training Comments

_____

_____

_____

Finishing Well

Jeff Hagen takes a view of goals similar to mine. The dentist from Washington State is no slacker. Few ultrarunners have won more often while aiming lower. In his 50s he does especially well in track races that last 24 or even 48 hours.

"I have always steered clear of setting lofty race goals," he says. "With them comes pressure, and if any little thing goes wrong—which is almost a certainty in any ultra event—I can easily become demoralized and perform poorly. By setting goals that are more achievable, if things happen to be going well, I sometimes adjust my goal upward during the second half of the event."

TRAINING TIP

Cruisers, consider eating on the run—especially if your marathon will last four hours or more. The most practical food is a sports gel, carried in a fanny-pack or plastic bag. Practice eating on the longest training run.

Dr. Hagen typically finishes his long races at a faster pace than he started them. He's seldom disappointed with his results.

Few runners lack motivation. Many are more likely to trip over the high hurdles of ambition. If high goals become hurdles that trip you up, try this: Divide the race into two parts, equal in size but very different in style. Run the first half of your race like a scientist, with careful planning and restraint. Then switch in the second half to running like an artist, creatively and emotionally.

Starting cautiously will often lead to finishing with a rush. Running the second half of a race faster than the first is misleadingly called *negative splits*. In fact, few feelings in this sport are more positive than a strong finish with an outcome that far exceeds expectations.

Date _____ *Plans* _____

Training Session

Type of run   □ long   □ fast   □ easy   □ none   □ race

Distance _____   **Time** _____

Pace _____ per mile   _____ per kilometer

Splits _____ / _____ / _____ / _____ / _____ / _____

Effort   □ max   □ hard   □ moderate   □ easy   □ rest

Training heart rates   target _____   actual _____

Warm-up _____   **Cool-down** _____   **Cross-training** _____

Training Conditions

Location _____   **Time of day** _____

People   □ alone   □ with group   □ race   □ with partner _____
                                                                              name

Surface   □ road   □ trail   □ track   □ mixed _____

Terrain   □ flat   □ hilly   □ mixed _____

Weather _____   **Shoes worn** _____

Diet   drinks during run _____   foods during run _____

Training Rating

Success level   10   9   8   7   6   5   4   3   2   1   0

Training Comments

_____

_____

_____

Honest Efforts

Running is a fundamentally honest sport. Runners as a group are basically honorable people. If we weren't, the sport would lose all meaning, because policing the efforts of hundreds or thousands of runners would be impossible.

You run a certain distance in a certain time, and that's the runner you are that day. Shortcutting the distance to improve your time is cheating, and for most of us committing such an act would be unthinkable.

But cheaters do creep out of hiding occasionally. (Think of Rosie Ruiz, whose "victory" at the 1980 Boston Marathon forever robbed the true winner, Jacqueline Gareau, of her most glorious moment.) When caught, they make news because they're so rare.

TRAINING TIP

Pacers and Racers, extend your longest training run to marathon length. Train as much *time* as you expect the marathon to take, even while going less than 26.2 miles (42.2K) because of the slower training pace.

At the 2001 New York City Marathon 99.99 percent of finishers ran the course honestly. A deviant tried to "finish" a race he hadn't run in full, but he was caught. We shook our heads in disgust as this "runner" (I can't bring myself to remove the quote marks) pulled a "Rosie" (so named for the most infamous of cheaters). There's no greater sin in this sport than trying to steal someone else's prize—and in this case, prize money.

Keith Dowling was the potential victim. The would-be thief attempted to run off with Dowling's $4,500 as the true fifth-place American at New York City. In sixth, Keith would have earned nothing. That was no harmless prank. It could have been prosecuted as a criminal act. I wish it had been, as an example that these rare acts are not only ethically but legally wrong.

Date _____ *Plans* _____

Training Session

Type of run   □ long   □ fast   □ easy   □ none   □ race

Distance _____   *Time* _____

Pace _____ per mile   _____ per kilometer

Splits _____ / _____ / _____ / _____ / _____ / _____

Effort   □ max   □ hard   □ moderate   □ easy   □ rest

Training heart rates target _____ actual _____

Warm-up _____ *Cool-down* _____ *Cross-training* _____

Training Conditions

Location _____   *Time of day* _____

People   □ alone   □ with group   □ race   □ with partner _____
name

Surface   □ road   □ trail   □ track   □ mixed _____

Terrain   □ flat   □ hilly   □ mixed _____

Weather _____   *Shoes worn* _____

Diet   drinks during run _____   foods during run _____

Training Rating

Success level   10   9   8   7   6   5   4   3   2   1   0

Training Comments

_____

_____

_____

═══ Would You Cheat? ═══

No charges have ever been filed, as far as I know, against cheaters in road races. But perpetrators such as the one who was exposed as a fraud at the 2001 New York City Marathon don't get away unpunished. This one forever branded himself as an outlaw against all that's honest in the sport. May he never again have the gall to show his face at a race. Exposure and exile will stop his cheating, if not make him repentant.

TRAINING TIP

Look how far you have come since the first week of this marathon program. The distance of your long run has jumped by more than 50 percent, and these distances might not seem any more imposing than the original ones did.

Our best defense against cheating is the healthy conscience of most runners. Few of us could live with a fraudulent race result.

My longest race was meant to be 100 miles (160K). It ended at 70 miles (113K), which still was my longest distance though I can't claim it as anything but a DNF (did not finish).

We ran that day on a multilap course with an out-and-back stretch at one end. It would have been possible to shortcut it by several blocks on each of the 40 laps.

I joked to fellow runner Peter Mattei, "Let's cut off this section. It's dark out here, and no one would see us. I won't tell if you won't."

This was no joking matter with Mattei. He said, "Someone would know I'd only run 97 miles [155K]. *I* would know, and I'd never be able to forgive myself."

Cheating is unimaginable when you think this way. And fortunately for us and for the sport as a whole, most runners do.

Date _____ *Plans* _____

Training Session

Type of run ☐ long ☐ fast ☐ easy ☐ none ☐ race

Distance _____ **Time** _____

Pace _____ per mile _____ per kilometer

Splits _____ / _____ / _____ / _____ / _____ / _____

Effort ☐ max ☐ hard ☐ moderate ☐ easy ☐ rest

Training heart rates target _____ actual _____

Warm-up _____ **Cool-down** _____ **Cross-training** _____

Training Conditions

Location _____ **Time of day** _____

People ☐ alone ☐ with group ☐ race ☐ with partner _____
name

Surface ☐ road ☐ trail ☐ track ☐ mixed _____

Terrain ☐ flat ☐ hilly ☐ mixed _____

Weather _____ **Shoes worn** _____

Diet drinks during run _____ foods during run _____

Training Rating

Success level 10 9 8 7 6 5 4 3 2 1 0

Training Comments

_____

_____

_____

Lesser Evils

We sometimes commit lesser sins than outright cheating without fully realizing they are sinful. I confess to having sinned in most of the ways described here, and maybe you have too:

- Exaggerating times. The older some runners are, the faster they were. Did I ever tell you about my marathon PR, set in the last century, of about 2:40 (meaning I once barely broke 2:49:59)?

- Running as an unregistered bandit. Sure, it's a public road. Go ahead and steal the services paid for by the number wearers.

- Wearing someone else's number. I heard of a man "borrowing" women's numbers, winning an award, and sending a young girl up to collect it "for my mother."

- Starting ahead of the starting line . . . or before the official starting time. You avoid congestion these ways. You also run less than the full distance or mess up the results.

- Entering a race "for the training" while never intending to go all the way or jumping in at midrace to pace someone. Planning to run less than full distance cheats against the spirit of racing.

- Shortening the course by crossing lawns or cutting through gas stations at corners. Shortcutting the prescribed route may lead to PRn'ts—fast times for substandard distances.

TRAINING TIP

Where, you ask, do the extra miles come from if your longest training run stops at 4 or more miles (6-plus kilometers) short of the marathon? Trust the magic of race day excitement to carry you the extra distance.

Confession to these and other past transgressions helps us to live with them and to go and sin no more. All are attacks on the basic self-policing honesty of the sport, and all are insults to the majority of runners who follow the honor code of the road.

Date _____ *Plans* _____

Training Session

Type of run ☐ long ☐ fast ☐ easy ☐ none ☐ race

Distance _____ *Time* _____

Pace _____ per mile _____ per kilometer

Splits _____ / _____ / _____ / _____ / _____ / _____

Effort ☐ max ☐ hard ☐ moderate ☐ easy ☐ rest

Training heart rates target _____ actual _____

Warm-up _____ *Cool-down* _____ *Cross-training* _____

Training Conditions

Location _____ *Time of day* _____

People ☐ alone ☐ with group ☐ race ☐ with partner _____
name

Surface ☐ road ☐ trail ☐ track ☐ mixed _____

Terrain ☐ flat ☐ hilly ☐ mixed _____

Weather _____ *Shoes worn* _____

Diet drinks during run _____ foods during run _____

Training Rating

Success level   10   9   8   7   6   5   4   3   2   1   0

Training Comments

_____

_____

_____

Visualize the race weekend scene as you head into the final premarathon weeks. Finalize both your running and travel plans.

GETTING AROUND

Your normal training ends this week, and it won't resume until well after the marathon. Think now, long before you journey to the race city, about the course you'll travel once you get there. Most important, how hilly is it, where are those hills, and how do you plan to deal with them? Choose your program from the options listed, assign runs to the next seven days of diary pages, and add details there for completed training.

Cruiser Program

Big day: Semilong run of 9 to 10 miles (15 to 16K), or half the distance of last week's long one. Run this distance nonstop with no walking breaks. Run slightly faster than your projected marathon pace.

Other training days: Three or four easy runs of 30 to 45 minutes each, with walking breaks optional.

Rest days: Two or three with no running, but possibly easy cross-training.

Pacer Program

Big day: Race of 5K to 10K or semilong run of 10 to 11 miles (16 to 18K), half of last week's long one, nonstop at your projected marathon pace or slightly faster.

Other training days: Four or five easy runs of 30 to 60 minutes each.

Rest days: One or two with no running, but possibly easy cross-training.

Racer Program

Long day: Semilong run of 11 to 12 miles (18 to 19K), or half the distance of last week's long one. Run at your projected marathon pace or slightly faster.

Fast day: Race of 5K to 10K, or 1- to 3-mile (1.6 to 5K) run at current 10K race pace. (This may be broken into shorter intervals that total 1 to 3 miles—1.6 to 5K—not counting recovery periods.) Warm up and cool down with easy running.

Other training days: Four easy runs of 30 to 60 minutes each.

Rest days: One with no running, but possibly easy cross-training.

See How We Run

I have one of the world's greatest jobs. On weekdays I write about runners. On weekends I see them at races.

My work takes me to dozens of races each year. Once I'm finished with the prerace talk that brought me there, the choice is mine—run in the race or stand by and cheer for other runners. Either way is equally satisfying, involving either receiving shouts of encouragement or giving them.

While I watch a race, my strategy is not to stand right at the finish line. You don't see the truth of the race there. If you can see anything through that crowd, it's a victory prance as runners celebrate the last steps of their day's work.

If you want to know what a race is really all about, then move a kilometer to a mile up the course. The view is clearer and closer there than at the finish line, the voices are quieter, and the views are more realistic.

First you see yourself in the other runners, and sometimes it isn't a pretty sight. You notice how long the wait is from the time the leaders pass until people of your ability appear. Then you think, *They look so much slower than I picture myself running at that pace.*

TRAINING TIP

Make final plans for race weekend, which is now less than three weeks away. Know how you'll get to the race city, when you'll arrive, and where you'll stay. Have the necessary reservations in hand.

Mostly, though, you see honest, concentrated, sometimes painful effort written on the faces and in the strides of the passing runners. Something in the way they look at this point makes bystanders shout support to strangers. Sometimes their words don't ring true. But the intentions behind them are always friendly and helpful.

Date _____ *Plans* _____

Training Session

Type of run   □ long   □ fast   □ easy   □ none   □ race

Distance _____   *Time* _____

Pace _____ per mile   _____ per kilometer

Splits _____ / _____ / _____ / _____ / _____ / _____

Effort   □ max   □ hard   □ moderate   □ easy   □ rest

Training heart rates   target _____   actual _____

Warm-up _____   *Cool-down* _____   *Cross-training* _____

Training Conditions

Location _____   *Time of day* _____

People   □ alone   □ with group   □ race   □ with partner _____
                                                                        name

Surface   □ road   □ trail   □ track   □ mixed _____

Terrain   □ flat   □ hilly   □ mixed _____

Weather _____   *Shoes worn* _____

Diet   drinks during run _____   foods during run _____

Training Rating

Success level   10   9   8   7   6   5   4   3   2   1   0

Training Comments

_____

_____

_____

Tell Me No Lies

Something in the look of the runners passing by the last stages of a marathon, and of their energy, makes the viewer tell them well-meaning lies. I've approached hundreds of finish lines and stood near hundreds more. I've always heard the same three lies and spoken them more than a few times myself:

- "You're almost there." Distance and time are elastic. When you're full of run, the early miles seem to pass in three minutes each, while the last mile can seem to stretch to half an hour. Distance can sometimes be truly variable as one viewer shouts, "You have less than a mile to go," then another one farther down the road informs you, "A little more than a mile to go."

- "It's all downhill from here." When you're weary, the topographical map loses all meaning. Downhills can seem like flat running, and the flats can feel uphill. True downhills are, at best, a mixed blessing because they add to the stress load on well-pounded legs. At this point, just stepping off a curb can be as jarring as leaping off a steeplechase barrier.

TRAINING TIP

Build a minivacation around the marathon, if possible. Plan to arrive early to shake off travel fatigue—especially if the trip involves a time-zone change—and arrange to linger for a day or two after the race.

- "Looking good." This is the perennial crowd favorite. You might look more relaxed and less tired than most of the people around you, but that's not the same as looking good. Don Kardong, Olympic-marathoner-turned-writer, once wrote, "Do you want to see how you'll look 20 years from now? Glance in a mirror right after you finish a marathon."

Date _____ *Plans* _____

Training Session

Type of run ☐ long ☐ fast ☐ easy ☐ none ☐ race

Distance _____ *Time* _____

Pace _____ per mile _____ per kilometer

Splits _____ / _____ / _____ / _____ / _____ / _____

Effort ☐ max ☐ hard ☐ moderate ☐ easy ☐ rest

Training heart rates target _____ actual _____

Warm-up _____ *Cool-down* _____ *Cross-training* _____

Training Conditions

Location _____ *Time of day* _____

People ☐ alone ☐ with group ☐ race ☐ with partner _____
name

Surface ☐ road ☐ trail ☐ track ☐ mixed _____

Terrain ☐ flat ☐ hilly ☐ mixed _____

Weather _____ *Shoes worn* _____

Diet drinks during run _____ foods during run _____

Training Rating

Success level   10   9   8   7   6   5   4   3   2   1   0

Training Comments

_____

_____

_____

Encouraging Words

Never, while nearing the finish line of a long race, do I expect to hear any spectators shout, "You have farther to go than you want to know." Or, "Look out for the killer hill between here and the finish line."

I have, though, had a rare truth-telling spectator ask me in the homestretch of the Royal Victoria Marathon, "Are you okay? You don't look so good." For him to say that, instead of the usual lie of "Looking good," I must have appeared in need of a 911 call.

Trust a New Yorker to be honest. A sign spotted at a point late in the New York City Marathon read, "Remember, you CHOSE to do this." And we even pay for the privilege of pushing ourselves this far, so no spectator needs to feel sorry for us.

TRAINING TIP

Wear used shoes. They should have passed the test of your longest run. It's too late now to change shoes, because you couldn't adequately break in and test the new ones.

When my turn comes to play cheerleader, I try to be both supportive and honest. My cheers stay neutral. "Way to go," I shout. Or maybe, "Good job." Or I just clap and then give a thumbs-up to anyone still able to make eye contact. I sometimes offer a hand to slap but seldom receive one in return. That's okay. I know that runners hear or notice the good wishes even when they don't acknowledge them.

It doesn't matter what an onlooker says, if anything. Runners only want to know that someone—friend or stranger, loud or silent—cares what they're doing.

Even when we aren't running ourselves, we still can play a big role in the race. We also participate by standing beside the road and supporting the passersby.

Date _____ *Plans* _____

Training Session

Type of run ☐ long ☐ fast ☐ easy ☐ none ☐ race

Distance _____ *Time* _____

Pace _____ per mile _____ per kilometer

Splits _____ / _____ / _____ / _____ / _____ / _____

Effort ☐ max ☐ hard ☐ moderate ☐ easy ☐ rest

Training heart rates target _____ actual _____

Warm-up _____ *Cool-down* _____ *Cross-training* _____

Training Conditions

Location _____ *Time of day* _____

People ☐ alone ☐ with group ☐ race ☐ with partner _____
  name

Surface ☐ road ☐ trail ☐ track ☐ mixed _____

Terrain ☐ flat ☐ hilly ☐ mixed _____

Weather _____ *Shoes worn* _____

Diet drinks during run _____ foods during run _____

Training Rating

Success level 10 9 8 7 6 5 4 3 2 1 0

Training Comments

_____

_____

_____

Standing By

This was their race day. It was my morning after. They rested the day before. I worked.

Their reason for being in Kelowna, British Columbia, was to run the Okanagan International Marathon or Half. Mine was to speak to them as a group and individually at the packet-pickup site.

They were now under way. I was two weeks past my latest marathon and happy to let them finish theirs this day.

My speaking work is great fun, but it still takes some effort. I have to get "up" for it, and a letdown inevitably follows. This feels something like the fuzzy-headed fatigue of the day after a race. As the runners left the start in Kelowna, I was left feeling disconnected from them.

TRAINING TIP

Peek again at the course map. Memorize the locations of hills (both ups and downs), key distance checkpoints, and aid stations. Decide also where family and friends can see you along the route.

I had no job to do now other than to clap and cheer at the finish. But this is one of the best services that anyone can offer a runner.

The runners began to arrive for their final lap around a dirt track. They started to give at least as much back to me in renewed enthusiasm as I did to them in final encouragement.

Walking the infield next to the track, I stood close enough to reach out and touch the passing runners. I knew few of them, and few showed any sign of knowing me.

I was simply a stranger reaching out to others in admiration and support. Their efforts moved me.

The best way to be moved is to be inspired. Marathoners silently say to spectators, "Come join us next time."

Date _____ **Plans** _____

Training Session

Type of run ☐ long ☐ fast ☐ easy ☐ none ☐ race

Distance _____ **Time** _____

Pace _____ per mile _____ per kilometer

Splits _____ / _____ / _____ / _____ / _____ / _____

Effort ☐ max ☐ hard ☐ moderate ☐ easy ☐ rest

Training heart rates target _____ actual _____

Warm-up _____ **Cool-down** _____ **Cross-training** _____

Training Conditions

Location _____ **Time of day** _____

People ☐ alone ☐ with group ☐ race ☐ with partner _____
name

Surface ☐ road ☐ trail ☐ track ☐ mixed _____

Terrain ☐ flat ☐ hilly ☐ mixed _____

Weather _____ **Shoes worn** _____

Diet drinks during run _____ foods during run _____

Training Rating

Success level 10 9 8 7 6 5 4 3 2 1 0

Training Comments

_____

_____

_____

Faces at the Races

The faces fascinated me as I watched them closely at the end of the Okanagan International Marathon in British Columbia. Smiling and pained faces . . . faces scrunched with effort and slack-jawed with fatigue . . . flushed and ashen faces . . . faces that made eye contact and those with the 26-mile stare.

Beyond the individual faces, I saw the face of the future. The look of this event was the youngest I'd seen in years and the most female ever at a race of this distance.

The sport has been graying for a long time. Young people haven't been attracted in great numbers to what they often view as a sport of their parents and grandparents.

"Other races in Canada and the U.S. still cater to the older runners, in their 40s and 50s," said John Stanton, president of the Running Room chain of stores that hosted this event. "Fifty-eight percent of runners in today's race are under 40." And almost one-quarter are in their 20s.

Women made up the majority of the young. In fact, women were the majority overall—with 53 percent of the field.

"Our Running Room clinics and marathons are not only doing the job of getting folks to the finish line," said Stanton. "We are also getting many who would not get there under some of the old training programs and old-style races. We are getting a whole new group running."

TRAINING TIP

Check your entry. You should have mailed it months ago, but has it been confirmed? If not, place a call or send an e-mail to the marathon office. Ask if your number will be mailed or if you pick it up on race weekend.

I looked into the fresh faces. They might be sending my age group and gender into eclipse, but I still liked what I saw.

Date _____ **Plans** _____

Training Session

Type of run   ☐ long   ☐ fast   ☐ easy   ☐ none   ☐ race

Distance _____   **Time** _____

Pace _____ per mile   _____ per kilometer

Splits _____ / _____ / _____ / _____ / _____ / _____

Effort   ☐ max   ☐ hard   ☐ moderate   ☐ easy   ☐ rest

Training heart rates target _____   actual _____

Warm-up _____   **Cool-down** _____   **Cross-training** _____

Training Conditions

Location _____   **Time of day** _____

People   ☐ alone   ☐ with group   ☐ race   ☐ with partner _____
                                                                         name

Surface   ☐ road   ☐ trail   ☐ track   ☐ mixed _____

Terrain   ☐ flat   ☐ hilly   ☐ mixed _____

Weather _____   **Shoes worn** _____

Diet   drinks during run _____   foods during run _____

Training Rating

Success level   10   9   8   7   6   5   4   3   2   1   0

Training Comments

_____

_____

_____

Shooting and Shouting

This race happened to have been a marathon in Las Vegas. But it could have been anyone's race, anywhere, and at any road distance. Race day involves not only you, the runner, but also the people who helped you get there and came to share in your final act.

I slipped out of the hotel room at five o'clock in the morning to catch a bus to the start a marathon's length outside of the city. Behind stayed my sleeping wife.

TRAINING TIP

Make this your last week of normal training before the marathon. And even now, with the countdown at little more than two weeks, your distance is dropping. Limit your big days this week to semilong and fast runs.

We had already made plans on when and where to meet again many hours later. She would leave the room at a reasonable hour, carrying instructions on how and when to find me on the course and at the finish line. We had been through this routine many times before. The well-tested plan went into action again in Las Vegas.

Barbara isn't a marathon runner herself, but she is a professional photographer and a savvy follower of our sport. She knew my expected pace and when it would bring me to meeting places along the course. We had plotted these spots in advance, and she had mapped how to reach them.

Her logistical task that day was tougher than mine. All I had to do was follow the crowd and the marked route. Barbara had to find her own way.

Our plan again worked beautifully. Barbara arrived at the designated spots on time, shot the necessary pictures, and shouted the needed encouragement, then was there to pick me up after the finish.

sy   □ none   □ race

_____ per kilometer

_____ / _____ / _____

□ easy   □ rest

ual _____

_____ **Cross-training** _____

me of day _____

th partner _____
                    name

mixed _____

_____

worn _____

during run _____

4   3   2   1   0

Tr

Suc

Trai

Viewer's Guide

1. Don't try to watch the start. The scene there is too crowded, and parking is too scarce. Let your runner walk a short distance, take the bus a long way, or be dropped off near the start with a good-luck hug or handshake.

2. Don't expect to drive on the course—or to bicycle there. It's either closed to traffic or should be. Don't risk interfering with runners by trying to take your car or bike onto or across the runners' route of travel.

3. Don't try to watch the finish. As with the start, this area is over-crowded. Unless you're the height of an NBA forward, or the race is a rarity with a grandstand for spectators, you won't see your favorite's final steps of the race.

4. Do plan to hit one or more points along the course. The race is long enough so that you can reach several spots by taking parallel and intersecting streets. Scout your route on a map, drive it in advance if possible, and plan arrival times at rendezvous points.

5. Do wait near the finish. Crowds thin out quickly as you leave that line, and even a few minutes' walk away you can stand within arm's length of the passing runners. Shoot your pictures, and shout loud and proud from there.

6. Do plan a meeting place. Rather than wade into the crowd searching for your runner, have him or her come to you at a prearranged spot. Then share the joy of a race well run.

TRAINING TIP

Stay extra alert to stress symptoms—a minor injury, the beginnings of a cold. Drop a scheduled run this week rather than risk an ailment that might stay with you through marathon day.

Date _____ *Plans* _____

Training Session

Type of run ☐ long ☐ fast ☐ easy ☐ none ☐ race

Distance _____ **Time** _____

Pace _____ per mile _____ per kilometer

Splits _____ / _____ / _____ / _____ / _____ / _____

Effort ☐ max ☐ hard ☐ moderate ☐ easy ☐ rest

Training heart rates target _____ actual _____

Warm-up _____ **Cool-down** _____ **Cross-training** _____

Training Conditions

Location _____ **Time of day** _____

People ☐ alone ☐ with group ☐ race ☐ with partner _____

name

Surface ☐ road ☐ trail ☐ track ☐ mixed _____

Terrain ☐ flat ☐ hilly ☐ mixed _____

Weather _____ **Shoes worn** _____

Diet drinks during run _____ foods during run _____

Training Rating

Success level 10 9 8 7 6 5 4 3 2 1 0

Training Comments

_____

_____

_____

Just as you trained up for the marathon, you must also ease down in the last weeks. This stores up energy and enthusiasm.

TAPERING OFF

Down comes your training to a final low-stress test of marathon pace and equipment. Run for one hour at the pace and in the shoes and clothes you've selected for race day. Otherwise you'll do little more than run easily and rest. As your training comes down, you can expect your energy and enthusiasm to rise and your nagging aches and pains to disappear. At the same time, however, it's normal to start imagining that you're coming down with a new illness or injury at the worst possible time. You probably aren't catching anything, but this is your mind's way of protecting you against training too much, too late. Choose your program from the options listed, assign runs to the next seven days of diary pages, and add details there for completed training.

Cruiser Program

Big day: Semilong run of one hour, covering whatever distance feels comfortable in that time.

Other training days: Three or four easy runs of 30 to 45 minutes each, with walking breaks optional.

Rest days: Two or three with no running, but possibly easy cross-training.

Pacer Program

Big day: Semilong run of one hour at marathon pace.

Other training days: Four or five easy runs of 30 to 60 minutes each.

Rest days: One or two with no running, but possibly easy cross-training.

Racer Program

Long day: Semilong run of one hour at marathon pace.

Fast day: 1- to 3-mile (1.6 to 5K) run at current 10K race pace. (This may be broken into shorter intervals that total 1 to 3 miles—1.6 to 5K—not counting recovery periods.) Warm up and cool down with easy running.

Other training days: Four easy runs of 30 to 60 minutes each.

Rest days: One with no running, but possibly easy cross-training.

Take Your Ease, Please

"**W**hat is your running routine?" This is one of the best questions one runner can ask another. Others are "How did you get so fast?" and "Can you give me advice on . . .?" and "Have you lost weight?"

"What do you run?" ranks among the best questions because it demands an honest answer. It doesn't ask what you once did or what you hope to do someday, but what you actually do now.

TRAINING TIP

Don't fret too much about your marathon prospects. If you have trained properly, if the long runs have reached planned length, and if you've stayed healthy, the race is all but guaranteed to go well.

Thanks, my fellow Oregonian Jerry Baker, for asking me by e-mail, "How much do you run?" My answer won't impress him or you, but neither is it a shameful little secret. My runs, measured by time instead of distance, average well below an hour apiece. The pace seldom rises out of the comfort zone.

A race still might lure me out of the comfort zone, but that happens rarely nowadays. I've raced as far and as fast as my ability and ambition will ever take me, and I have nothing left to prove on the outer limits of effort. Easy running is my home base, and I'm content to spend most of my days there.

Easy is one of the least-used words in a runner's vocabulary, if it's not actually spoken as a four-letter word. We talk the least about the runs we take most often, the easy ones. That's because all the accolades in this sport reward the big efforts. These words tend to end in *-est*—*fastest, longest, toughest, best*. But after every *-est* must come many *easys*.

Hard runs are essential because racing is hard. But easy runs also matter because they make the hard ones possible.

Date _____ *Plans* _____

Training Session

Type of run ☐ long ☐ fast ☐ easy ☐ none ☐ race

Distance _____ **Time** _____

Pace _____ per mile _____ per kilometer

Splits _____ / _____ / _____ / _____ / _____ / _____

Effort ☐ max ☐ hard ☐ moderate ☐ easy ☐ rest

Training heart rates target _____ actual _____

Warm-up _____ **Cool-down** _____ **Cross-training** _____

Training Conditions

Location _____ **Time of day** _____

People ☐ alone ☐ with group ☐ race ☐ with partner _____
                                                                  name

Surface ☐ road ☐ trail ☐ track ☐ mixed _____

Terrain ☐ flat ☐ hilly ☐ mixed _____

Weather _____ **Shoes worn** _____

Diet drinks during run _____ foods during run _____

Training Rating

Success level   10   9   8   7   6   5   4   3   2   1   0

Training Comments

_____

_____

_____

In Praise of Easy

No prize in running is awarded for going easier. No one boasts, "I ran an easy 3 miles [5K] today," or pats your back for miles or kilometers run two minutes slower than race pace. No one writes books on how to run SSD—short, slow distance. No one gives speeches praising runs so undemanding that first-year runners can do them in their sleep.

No, we don't talk much about runs that are neither long nor fast. Or when they do come up in runners' conversations, we call them by assumed names. One alternative definition is particularly distasteful—*junk miles*. What can be trashy about runs that are vital ingredients in the training mix?

TRAINING TIP

Consider what causes bad marathons. Mostly it's running too little or too much distance in training. Another common source of problems occurs in the tapering period: running too much, too late.

The occasional long run must be long enough to prepare you for your longest race (for a marathon in your current case). The infrequent fast run must be fast enough to train you for your shortest race. So too must the many easy runs be easy enough to heal the pains of the hard days. Easy runs are the twine that binds together the hard runs. Without the easy days, the good health that supports all running can come unraveled.

Easy runs are accurately called "recovery" or "active rest." They're known as "filler" between hard days or as "token runs." I think of these as "gentle runs" because they're more soothing than demanding. And I sometimes call them "dog runs," both because my four-legged friend goes along and because I'm dogging the effort.

Date _____ **Plans** _____

Training Session

Type of run   □ long   □ fast   □ easy   □ none   □ race

Distance _____   **Time** _____

Pace _____ per mile   _____ per kilometer

Splits _____ / _____ / _____ / _____ / _____ / _____

Effort   □ max   □ hard   □ moderate   □ easy   □ rest

Training heart rates   target _____   actual _____

Warm-up _____   **Cool-down** _____   **Cross-training** _____

Training Conditions

Location _____   **Time of day** _____

People   □ alone   □ with group   □ race   □ with partner _____
                                                                        name

Surface   □ road   □ trail   □ track   □ mixed _____

Terrain   □ flat   □ hilly   □ mixed _____

Weather _____   **Shoes worn** _____

Diet   drinks during run _____   foods during run _____

Training Rating

Success level   10   9   8   7   6   5   4   3   2   1   0

Training Comments

_____

_____

_____

What's Easy?

Putting numbers on the definition of *easy*, I've long thought that if my slow runs last less than an hour, they qualify as easy. Truly easy runs would average closer to a *half*-hour.

Dr. Kenneth Cooper, of aerobics fame, recommends easy runs of 2 to 3 miles (3 to 5K). His research indicates that runners can gain and maintain basic aerobic fitness at this level while minimizing injury risk.

However you define these little runs, they must feel neither long nor fast. Whatever numbers you put on them, they must be short and slow enough to repeat day after day without running yourself down.

TRAINING TIP

Don't try to pack in extra training in the last week or two. It won't help. Nothing you do in training now will make your marathon better. But it's not too late to make it worse. It's never too late to hurt yourself.

George Sheehan, the late *Runner's World* columnist, defined his easy runs by what they weren't as well as by what they were: "not a test but a therapy, not a trial but a reward." Easy runs reward you for running hard. Just as you can't appreciate a meal unless you're hungry or a shower unless you're dirty, you can't know how good an easy run can feel until you've gone hard.

If hard runs are the most you can endure, easy ones are the least you will accept. Easy is what you run while making plans for your next hard day.

Getting on with these little runs is just as important as getting up for the big ones. I say *more* important because "hard" is a nice place to visit from time to time, but "easy" is where you live out most of your days.

Date _____ *Plans* _____

Training Session

Type of run ☐ long ☐ fast ☐ easy ☐ none ☐ race

Distance _____ *Time* _____

Pace _____ per mile _____ per kilometer

Splits _____ / _____ / _____ / _____ / _____ / _____

Effort ☐ max ☐ hard ☐ moderate ☐ easy ☐ rest

Training heart rates target _____ actual _____

Warm-up _____ *Cool-down* _____ *Cross-training* _____

Training Conditions

Location _____ *Time of day* _____

People ☐ alone ☐ with group ☐ race ☐ with partner _____

name

Surface ☐ road ☐ trail ☐ track ☐ mixed _____

Terrain ☐ flat ☐ hilly ☐ mixed _____

Weather _____ *Shoes worn* _____

Diet drinks during run _____ foods during run _____

Training Rating

Success level 10 9 8 7 6 5 4 3 2 1 0

Training Comments

_____

_____

_____

Rest of the Week

Where I came from, which is small-town Iowa, we had mixed feelings about Sundays. This mixture extended to my own family.

Sunday was the Biblical day of rest. My mother observed it, refusing to indulge in any commercial or entertainment venture on Sundays and urging her children to abstain as well. My father couldn't rest that day, or any day. He was a farmer, and the animals didn't abstain from eating on the seventh day.

As a runner I took after Dad, not Mom. For years I ran seven days every week. Skipping a day of running would have been like fasting one-seventh of the time.

In my youth, not outgrown until my early 40s, I was a streaker. Years passed between days off, and those were never voluntary. Little short of hospitalization would make me rest.

TRAINING TIP

Realize that training has a delayed-reaction effect. You don't draw your ability to run a marathon from what you run this week but from a reservoir of fitness filled weeks and months earlier.

Then I started stopping by choice, becoming a born-again believer in rest. Like many converts to a new theology, I went from one extreme to another: from never missing a day to never running more than a couple of days straight.

I ran by "cycles"—a three-day round of longer run, faster run, and rest . . . or, alternatively, one rest day for every hour of running. I even wrote, "There's no such thing as an 'easy' run. The best way to recover is to rest"—which I did two or three days every week. This was too many, and it had to change. Running this seldom left me feeling like a lost soul of a runner.

Runners want to run. Even a short, slow run can be easier to take than no run.

Date _____ *Plans* _____

Training Session

Type of run   □ long   □ fast   □ easy   □ none   □ race

Distance _____ *Time* _____

Pace _____ per mile   _____ per kilometer

Splits _____ / _____ / _____ / _____ / _____ / _____

Effort   □ max   □ hard   □ moderate   □ easy   □ rest

Training heart rates target _____ actual _____

Warm-up _____ *Cool-down* _____ *Cross-training* _____

Training Conditions

Location _____ *Time of day* _____

People □ alone   □ with group   □ race   □ with partner _____
name

Surface   □ road   □ trail   □ track   □ mixed _____

Terrain   □ flat   □ hilly   □ mixed _____

Weather _____ *Shoes worn* _____

Diet   drinks during run _____   foods during run _____

Training Rating

Success level   10   9   8   7   6   5   4   3   2   1   0

Training Comments

_____

_____

_____

Day Off

Tom Mann set me straight when this longtime runner from California wrote, "My running has gone through a wonderful six months or so of really feeling like a runner again. I shed some ugly pounds, started doing a little (very little) speed training and went back to doing some running every day. Within two weeks I was like a new person."

After hearing from Tom, I slipped into a new pattern: six days of running each week—one big day (longer or faster than normal) and all the others easy except one.

I now rest one day most weeks. This usually is on a Sunday, though exceptions are allowed. A harder-than-normal Saturday, my typical long-run day, might extend the rest to Monday and beyond. Or I might rest on Saturday for a Sunday race, then rest again afterward.

TRAINING TIP

Go into the race well rested by allowing at least two weeks of gradually dwindling effort. Extra-hard work in these final days does nothing but drain your energy pool at the worst possible time.

This weekly pattern finally brings me into step with the tradition most other runners observe. They've long taken a big day and a rest day on their weekends. Now so do I.

Most weeks, Sunday is my day off. It's necessary, not only to keep me from backsliding into the habits of the streaker, but also because this is often a travel day when I'm on the road for work and a family day when I'm home. Sunday also serves as a day for pausing to reflect on the running of the week past and to recharge for one coming up.

I haven't exactly found religion but have adopted a day of rest. My mother would approve.

Date _____ **Plans** _____

Training Session

Type of run   ☐ long   ☐ fast   ☐ easy   ☐ none   ☐ race

Distance _____   **Time** _____

Pace _____ per mile   _____ per kilometer

Splits _____ / _____ / _____ / _____ / _____ / _____

Effort   ☐ max   ☐ hard   ☐ moderate   ☐ easy   ☐ rest

Training heart rates   target _____   actual _____

Warm-up _____   **Cool-down** _____   **Cross-training** _____

Training Conditions

Location _____   **Time of day** _____

People   ☐ alone   ☐ with group   ☐ race   ☐ with partner _____
name

Surface   ☐ road   ☐ trail   ☐ track   ☐ mixed _____

Terrain   ☐ flat   ☐ hilly   ☐ mixed _____

Weather _____   **Shoes worn** _____

Diet   drinks during run _____   foods during run _____

Training Rating

Success level   10   9   8   7   6   5   4   3   2   1   0

Training Comments

_____

_____

_____

Out of Work

Some of my best friends are editors. They are the people who make their living by polishing other people's writing.

Editors run in my family—father, sister, daughter. I've done some editing myself but now am more an "editee."

As a writer I appreciate the many editors who have made me look better when my writing goes public. But this doesn't mean we don't sometimes quibble over word changes. I've spent a career trying not to use certain words. I cringe when they show up under my byline. *Workout* is one such word. I don't like it and don't write it. When an editor inserts it, I ask that the simple word *run* replace it. This happened to one of my magazine columns when a proof copy of an article came to me littered with *workouts.* I requested and received all the changes.

TRAINING TIP

Run minimal amounts in the last week or two before the marathon, and plan to rest completely the final day or two. Save the trained-in strength for the biggest day, when you need it most.

But we both forgot to re-edit a sidebar that went with the article. All the unused W-words landed there—one in the headline and five more in just two published paragraphs. Why does it matter? Because how we describe an activity shapes our view of it.

I haven't thought of running as work since high school. A coach named Hi Covey taught me to use a different word. Covey, my home state of Iowa's most successful coach, thought of *work* and *workout* as "dreary words that call up negative images. If I talked all the time about how hard running is, who would want to do it?"

Work is something we're required to do. Running is what we choose to do in off-work hours.

Date _____ **Plans** _____

Training Session

Type of run ☐ long ☐ fast ☐ easy ☐ none ☐ race

Distance _____ **Time** _____

Pace _____ per mile _____ per kilometer

Splits _____ / _____ / _____ / _____ / _____ / _____

Effort ☐ max ☐ hard ☐ moderate ☐ easy ☐ rest

Training heart rates target _____ actual _____

Warm-up _____ **Cool-down** _____ **Cross-training** _____

Training Conditions

Location _____ **Time of day** _____

People ☐ alone ☐ with group ☐ race ☐ with partner _____
                                                                  name

Surface ☐ road ☐ trail ☐ track ☐ mixed _____

Terrain ☐ flat ☐ hilly ☐ mixed _____

Weather _____ **Shoes worn** _____

Diet drinks during run _____ foods during run _____

Training Rating

Success level 10 9 8 7 6 5 4 3 2 1 0

Training Comments

_____

_____

_____

Not Working

Calling running *work* implies doing it because you have to but don't really want to. It suggests putting up with a distasteful task now so that you can earn a payoff later.

But what if that payday never comes, or it's smaller than expected? Would you think that all your time and effort had gone to waste?

Running isn't a second job. No one pays us or forces us to do it. Running is a hobby. A challenging hobby, to be sure, but not work in the way we usually define the word.

We could take vocabulary lessons from other sports. Basketball and baseball, tennis and golf aren't worked; they're *played*.

TRAINING TIP

Expect any of your physical ailments to magnify as the marathon approaches. Imaginary problems become real, and small ones grow large. Also expect them to do no real damage and to vanish when the race begins.

America's all-time greatest running coach talked his athletes out of thinking of their runs in terms of hard labor. Bill Bowerman told about a banker friend of his "who doesn't feel he has 'worked' a day in his life because he enjoys banking so much. A banker must practice banking virtually 12 months a year. Runners must do the same with their running. If they don't do that and don't enjoy it, they're never going to reach the top. Well, they may not reach the top anyway. But if they enjoy the running, they are getting one of its biggest prizes."

When you run, don't be like a worker who counts the hours till quitting time, the days till the weekend, the weeks till vacation, the years till retirement. Always working toward distant finish lines may mean missing the fun in being where you are now.

Date _____ *Plans* _____

Training Session

Type of run ☐ long ☐ fast ☐ easy ☐ none ☐ race

Distance _____ *Time* _____

Pace _____ per mile _____ per kilometer

Splits _____ / _____ / _____ / _____ / _____ / _____

Effort ☐ max ☐ hard ☐ moderate ☐ easy ☐ rest

Training heart rates target _____ actual _____

Warm-up _____ *Cool-down* _____ *Cross-training* _____

Training Conditions

Location _____ *Time of day* _____

People ☐ alone ☐ with group ☐ race ☐ with partner _____
                                                         name

Surface ☐ road ☐ trail ☐ track ☐ mixed _____

Terrain ☐ flat ☐ hilly ☐ mixed _____

Weather _____ *Shoes worn* _____

Diet drinks during run _____ foods during run _____

Training Rating

Success level   10   9   8   7   6   5   4   3   2   1   0

Training Comments

_____

_____

_____

Training done in the final days does you no good. So you relax then, trusting what you did weeks and months earlier.

RESTING UP

Nothing you do this week can train you any better for the marathon. It's too late for that. However, it's never too late to undermine your race by trying to cram in last-minute work. Don't stop running completely in this final week, which could throw you too far off your routine. But limit yourself to easy runs (even easier than during a normal week), while taking an extra day or two of rest. This also could be your travel week. Arrive in the marathon city soon enough to recover from the trip, deal with any jet lag, preview the course, pick up your race packet, and spend some time sampling the excitement that a marathon weekend has to offer. Choose your program from the following options, assign runs to the next seven days of diary pages, and add details there for completed training.

Cruiser Program

Big day: None.

Other training days: Three or four easy runs of about 30 minutes each, with walking breaks optional.

Rest days: Three or four with no running, but possibly easy cross-training early in the week.

Pacer Program

Big day: None.

Other training days: Four or five easy runs of about 30 minutes each.

Rest days: Two or three with no running, but possibly easy cross-training early in the week.

Racer Program

Long day: None.

Fast day: None, but possibly some light speed training in easy runs.

Other training days: Four to six easy runs of about 30 minutes each.

Rest days: One to three with no running, but possibly easy cross-training early in the week.

Code of the Road

Please don't misread what I'm about to say. I love seeing races fill to overflowing with runners, run-walkers, and even pure walkers. I'm not about to say that only the fast few should race and everyone else should step aside and watch.

What must be said, though, is that crowds create problems. Running in peak midpack traffic at races, I see too many infractions of race rules and violations of common courtesy. Minor wrongs grow into major disruptions when hundreds or thousands of people commit them.

In these crowds, too many runners act like drivers veering to an exit ramp without looking or signaling. Running becomes a contact sport. This isn't the fault of race organizers. Officials can only do so much crowd controlling. The crowds must largely control themselves by following a code of the road written into the traditions of the sport.

TRAINING TIP

Find out what the on-course drinks will be and where they'll be available. If they are the wrong type or there aren't enough of them, make private plans for special delivery of your liquids.

The problem is, newbie and once-a-year runners haven't spent enough time in the sport to memorize this code. Most displays of bad running etiquette come from innocence or ignorance of these customs, not malicious intent.

So widespread is the problem that the Road Runners Club of America appointed one of its officers, Freddi Carlip, to serve as "Ms. Road Manners." She makes appearances and writes columns on these issues.

Big road races resemble rush-hour traffic. Both move better and take you where you want to go faster when you follow certain rules and customs. Observe them yourself and let others know, politely, when they stray from these traditional practices of road racing.

Date _____ **Plans** _____

Training Session

Type of run ☐ long ☐ fast ☐ easy ☐ none ☐ race

Distance _____ **Time** _____

Pace _____ per mile _____ per kilometer

Splits _____ / _____ / _____ / _____ / _____ / _____

Effort ☐ max ☐ hard ☐ moderate ☐ easy ☐ rest

Training heart rates target _____ actual _____

Warm-up _____ **Cool-down** _____ **Cross-training** _____

Training Conditions

Location _____ **Time of day** _____

People ☐ alone ☐ with group ☐ race ☐ with partner _____

name

Surface ☐ road ☐ trail ☐ track ☐ mixed _____

Terrain ☐ flat ☐ hilly ☐ mixed _____

Weather _____ **Shoes worn** _____

Diet drinks during run _____ foods during run _____

Training Rating

Success level 10 9 8 7 6 5 4 3 2 1 0

Training Comments

_____

_____

_____

Mannerly Running

1. Leave children, dogs, and well-meaning friends on the sidelines. Baby Joggers and leashed pets create hazards for the runners around you. So do supporters accompanying you on bicycles or in-line skates, or those who dash into the streets to hug or run along with you.

2. Start where you expect to finish. Know what the pace signs mean. Never start in front of the starting line or before the official starting time, which both give false results.

3. Run in a straight line whenever possible. Look before you veer (or spit, or blow your nose), and don't change lanes unless you're two steps in front of the nearest runner. If you take the increasingly popular walking breaks, walk to the side of the road.

4. Run side-by-side with no more than one companion. Don't create a multiperson roadblock for the runners behind you, especially when your group stops as one for a walk or a drink.

TRAINING TIP

Plan your last meal—what and when? Order the same foods you have eaten trouble-free before your long runs. Allow the same amount of time between that meal and the marathon as you did when training long.

5. Take out your own trash if you carried any bars or gels to consume along the way. Don't toss down the wrappers as if Mom would come along later to pick up after you. (Drink cups aren't your responsibility because the race supplies them.)

6. If you have a complaint about the event's conduct, don't address it to the low-level volunteers who are most visible. Don't discourage them from ever wanting to work at a race again. Take your complaint to the race director—preferably in writing after the heat of race day has eased for both of you.

Date _____ **Plans** _____

Training Session

Type of run   ☐ long   ☐ fast   ☐ easy   ☐ none   ☐ race

Distance _____ **Time** _____

Pace _____ per mile   _____ per kilometer

Splits _____ / _____ / _____ / _____ / _____ / _____

Effort   ☐ max   ☐ hard   ☐ moderate   ☐ easy   ☐ rest

Training heart rates target _____ actual _____

Warm-up _____ **Cool-down** _____ **Cross-training** _____

Training Conditions

Location _____ **Time of day** _____

People ☐ alone   ☐ with group   ☐ race   ☐ with partner _____
                                                                        name

Surface   ☐ road   ☐ trail   ☐ track   ☐ mixed _____

Terrain   ☐ flat   ☐ hilly   ☐ mixed _____

Weather _____ **Shoes worn** _____

Diet   drinks during run _____   foods during run _____

Training Rating

Success level   10   9   8   7   6   5   4   3   2   1   0

Training Comments

_____

_____

_____

Making Memories

Arun is such a nice way to start a day that I've started more than 15,000 days like this. Most of these routine runs were worth repeating, but few have been memorable.

Already I can barely recall where this morning's run took me. It was too easy and pleasant to remember for long. Like footsteps on a dry road, it left behind nothing to distinguish it from thousands of other runs.

Of all the days in a career, a tiny percentage go into the mental video library. Here the pictures and words forever stay as clear as the day they went onto tape.

My most memorable days are all race days. What I remember first about them is that they were not much fun until they were done. Racing at its best never is.

TRAINING TIP

Unless you intend to race with the leaders, forget about doing any warm-up running. Save every step for the marathon, and warm up over the first few miles or kilometers as you settle into your pace.

Running can be great fun in all ways that runners define the word. Fun is running through the woods on an October afternoon, hearing leaves crunch underfoot. Fun is leaving the first footsteps in new snow on a January morning. Fun is the first stripping to shorts in spring or the first baring of shoulders to the sun in summer. Fun is joining a partner or a group and easing the miles with your conversation. Fun is going into a run or race with no goal, thereby leaving yourself open to surprises and immune to disappointments.

Everyday runs can be joyful in and of themselves. But memories so easily and often won are short-lived.

Date _____ **Plans** _____

Training Session

Type of run   □ long   □ fast   □ easy   □ none   □ race

Distance _____   **Time** _____

Pace _____ per mile   _____ per kilometer

Splits _____ / _____ / _____ / _____ / _____ / _____

Effort   □ max   □ hard   □ moderate   □ easy   □ rest

Training heart rates target _____   actual _____

Warm-up _____ **Cool-down** _____ **Cross-training** _____

Training Conditions

Location _____   **Time of day** _____

People   □ alone   □ with group   □ race   □ with partner _____
name

Surface   □ road   □ trail   □ track   □ mixed _____

Terrain   □ flat   □ hilly   □ mixed _____

Weather _____   **Shoes worn** _____

Diet   drinks during run _____   foods during run _____

Training Rating

Success level   10   9   8   7   6   5   4   3   2   1   0

Training Comments

_____

_____

_____

Meeting the Beast

The race, if run with great effort and high expectations, is not much fun before and little fun during. It is a beast to be fought.

You hate the thought of going into battle, but you know you must. If you retreat, the beast wins by default because your nerve has failed before your strength is tested. This battle brings moments of panic and pain, but not to try would feel worse. I've found no cure for these feelings. They stretch from my earliest track races to my latest marathons.

TRAINING TIP

Start with the intention of making the first (warm-up) mile or kilometer your slowest of the day. You probably have no choice while fighting the crowd, but don't let the early slowness trouble you. You'll soon be up to speed.

Recently I uncovered a more than 40-year-old newspaper clipping. Now yellowed and brittle, its headline and byline are missing, and the years have washed away many of the words. Little more than the molecules of memory hold the story together, but they preserve the finest details from that day.

Before the race the reporter had asked, "How do you feel?" That old story has me saying, "Terrible. I don't know how I'll do." I feared not doing what had to be done that day.

Little is at stake in my current marathons. I've run this far dozens of times before and have run much faster than current times. Still, I never fail to suffer from advanced premarathon anxiety.

In the last week before a race each little tweak in my legs, tickle in my throat, or twinge in my gut threatens to blow up into a major illness or injury. This magnification of symptoms is normal and expected.

These worries have nothing to do with the actual discomfort of the injury or illness. They're fears of not being able to experience the discomfort of racing.

Date _____ **Plans** _____

Training Session

Type of run ☐ long ☐ fast ☐ easy ☐ none ☐ race

Distance _____ **Time** _____

Pace _____ per mile _____ per kilometer

Splits _____ / _____ / _____ / _____ / _____ / _____

Effort ☐ max ☐ hard ☐ moderate ☐ easy ☐ rest

Training heart rates target _____ actual _____

Warm-up _____ **Cool-down** _____ **Cross-training** _____

Training Conditions

Location _____ **Time of day** _____

People ☐ alone ☐ with group ☐ race ☐ with partner _____
                                                                          name

Surface ☐ road ☐ trail ☐ track ☐ mixed _____

Terrain ☐ flat ☐ hilly ☐ mixed _____

Weather _____ **Shoes worn** _____

Diet drinks during run _____ foods during run _____

Training Rating

Success level   10   9   8   7   6   5   4   3   2   1   0

Training Comments

_____

_____

_____

Harder the Better

Doubts peak in the last hour before a big race—especially a marathon because it is such a long race. You have a big, long-lasting job to do and are as likely to fail as succeed at it.

Yes, every marathoner who finishes is a winner. But there's no guarantee before the marathon starts that you'll finish it.

You can't know in advance how the race will end, which is why racing is both fascinating and fearsome. This fear, unpleasant as it feels at the time, is good for you because it brings out your best efforts.

In my present-day marathons, PMS (premarathon syndrome) is still a necessary part of the experience—the mind's way of readying the body for the hard work ahead. The imagined maladies always melt away in the first half-hour, leaving me to worry about the normal challenges of the marathon, which are tall enough.

TRAINING TIP

Time yourself. Click on your watch only as you cross the starting line (not when the gun sounds). This way you ensure more accurate splits and final time than the "official" clock shows.

A race well run brings instant relief from all the work and worry. That's when the fun of racing begins, at the finish line.

A news story from the 1960s tells of me "looking fresh . . . bouncing around congratulating the other runners." The fun had already started and would never stop.

Taking on this beast, racing, and fighting the good fight push the after-joy to a level no routine run can leave behind. You suffer for this joy, and it stays with you long after the wounds of extreme effort heal. The mental videotapes from your scariest, hardest, and best days are indestructible.

Date _____ **Plans** _____

Training Session

Type of run ☐ long ☐ fast ☐ easy ☐ none ☐ race

Distance _____ **Time** _____

Pace _____ per mile _____ per kilometer

Splits _____ / _____ / _____ / _____ / _____ / _____

Effort ☐ max ☐ hard ☐ moderate ☐ easy ☐ rest

Training heart rates target _____ actual _____

Warm-up _____ **Cool-down** _____ **Cross-training** _____

Training Conditions

Location _____ **Time of day** _____

People ☐ alone ☐ with group ☐ race ☐ with partner _____
                                                                       name

Surface ☐ road ☐ trail ☐ track ☐ mixed _____

Terrain ☐ flat ☐ hilly ☐ mixed _____

Weather _____ **Shoes worn** _____

Diet drinks during run _____ foods during run _____

Training Rating

Success level   10   9   8   7   6   5   4   3   2   1   0

Training Comments

_____

_____

_____

Chasing Dreams

Desmond O'Neill numbers himself among a rare breed of runners: those who started in the 1950s and are coming to their half-century mark in the sport. He told me, "I still dream of finding the 'perfect' running shoe. It's a good recurring running dream, even if it never comes true.

"The nightmare running dream is arriving at the start of a race either late, or without my shoes, or both. Do you ever have dreams or nightmares about running?"

TRAINING TIP

Divide the marathon into equal parts. Feel that you're holding back in the first half when the natural urge is to speed up and when runners around you are struggling to pass you. Let them go.

Oh, do I! At the risk of exposing the darkest reaches of my mind, I'll confess to a few to see if they trigger any nods of recognition in you.

One dream came to me twice at the Royal Victoria Marathon—first in my sleeping mind and then for real. The prerace dream had me needing a ride to the starting line. We found all four of our car's tires flat.

I told my wife, Barbara, about the dream. Her instant interpretation: "You're worried about your feet giving out, or maybe just about feeling flat and tired."

My marathon wound down into a survival shuffle. I hoped to see Barbara at 25 miles (40K), because I'd rehearsed a greeting for her. "I'm flat and tired," I would say, "but not *re*tired."

We missed connections late in that race, but it's just as well she didn't see me. Such shuffling isn't a pretty sight in a loved one.

Eventually I finished. The memories of that day are better than the dreams were the night before.

Date _____ *Plans* _____

Training Session

Type of run □ long   □ fast   □ easy   □ none   □ race

Distance _____   **Time** _____

Pace _____ per mile   _____ per kilometer

Splits _____ / _____ / _____ / _____ / _____ / _____

Effort   □ max   □ hard   □ moderate   □ easy   □ rest

Training heart rates target _____   actual _____

Warm-up _____   **Cool-down** _____   **Cross-training** _____

Training Conditions

Location _____   **Time of day** _____

People □ alone   □ with group   □ race   □ with partner _____
name

Surface   □ road   □ trail   □ track   □ mixed _____

Terrain   □ flat   □ hilly   □ mixed _____

Weather _____   **Shoes worn** _____

Diet   drinks during run _____   foods during run _____

Training Rating

Success level   10   9   8   7   6   5   4   3   2   1   0

Training Comments

_____

_____

_____

Dream On

Many of my running dreams deal with frustrations: can't find the starting line . . . can't get my shoes on . . . can't pin on my number . . . can't set my watch to 0:00 . . . can't find my way on a course that passes through the maze-like corridors and closed doors of office buildings or hotels. A student of dreams would have to tell me what all this means. It may have to do with fears of ambitions being blocked.

TRAINING TIP

Run the second half of your marathon much differently than the first. Push on when your natural urge is to slow down. Take pleasure in passing the people who passed you earlier.

Rich Englehart, a professor of psychology as well as a running dreamer, says, "Most dreams are related to memories or to anticipation of impending events. I'd expect some of the 'can't find shoes' or 'missed connection' dreams have to do with anticipation and anxiety over an impending race or over a task that seems racelike in your understanding."

My oldest dreams go back to nights before high school and college races, when sleep came fitfully and made the dreamscape easier to replay. My legs turned to cooked spaghetti and wouldn't support me. I wound up "running" on all fours.

The "crawling" dream rarely surfaces anymore. Now that I'm truly slow, I more often dream about being really fast, running with the leaders but always waking up before finishing. This may have to do with what I imagine to be potential never tapped.

Another old standby dream reappeared the night before I wrote these lines. While headed into a crowd of runners, I looked down to see that I'd forgotten to wear shorts. What does that tell you, Dr. Freud?

Date _____ **Plans** _____

Training Session

Type of run □ long □ fast □ easy □ none □ race

Distance _____ **Time** _____

Pace _____ per mile _____ per kilometer

Splits _____ / _____ / _____ / _____ / _____ / _____

Effort □ max □ hard □ moderate □ easy □ rest

Training heart rates target _____ actual _____

Warm-up _____ **Cool-down** _____ **Cross-training** _____

Training Conditions

Location _____ **Time of day** _____

People □ alone □ with group □ race □ with partner _____

name

Surface □ road □ trail □ track □ mixed _____

Terrain □ flat □ hilly □ mixed _____

Weather _____ **Shoes worn** _____

Diet drinks during run _____ foods during run _____

Training Rating

Success level 10 9 8 7 6 5 4 3 2 1 0

Training Comments

_____

_____

_____

Marathon day will leave you with mental pictures that last a lifetime. Do your best to make sure these are pleasant memories.

DOING IT

It's here at last. Three months after you entered this program, you reach graduation day. This is the culmination of all that you've planned, worked for, worried about. This weekend, you become a marathoner for the first time, or you rewrite your personal record, or you climb higher on the list of finishers, or you add to your count of finishes.

Unlike all other chapters in the book, this one covers only two days. The first is marathon day. You know all about what needs to be done then. But you might not have thought much about the next day, which is just as important—if somewhat less exciting. This is when you travel home and take bows for your marathon result, when you savor all that you've done, when you nurse your sore muscles, and most of all when you start recovering.

The quickest and best way to recover is by avoiding the activity that caused the damage. Don't try to run out the soreness; rest it. Eat more than usual, drink more, brag more, sit more, sleep more. But don't run at all the day after your marathon. In fact, hold off doing any further running until the pain and stiffness ease. Choose your program from the list of options, assign runs to the next two days of diary pages, and add details there for completed running.

Cruiser Program

Big day: Cruise the marathon, running at the pace you've projected and taking walking breaks as you've practiced them.

Rest day: No running on the day after the marathon.

Pacer Program

Big day: Pace the marathon, running at the tempo you've projected and keeping walking breaks as an option.

Rest day: No running on the day after the marathon.

Racer Program

Big day: Race the marathon at the pace you've projected.

Rest day: No running on the day after the marathon.

Waiting and Worrying

Feeling like a second-class marathon citizen, I went straight to the back of the yellow school bus that would carry runners to the start of the Las Vegas Marathon. Sitting in the last seat was a tall Latino man of maybe 30. He stood up and let me squeeze into the window seat. I could hear him worrying that his long legs would cramp, and he wanted to stretch them into the aisle.

I got him to talk so that he would fret less. He introduced himself as Manuel and said, "I ran a 3:45 marathon two months ago and am shooting for 3:15 today." No wonder he looked scared.

We arrived at the starting line two hours before race time. Manuel bolted from the bus, as did most of the other adrenaline-poisoned passengers. Shadowy figures warmed up on the desert road. Lines formed at the forest of portable toilets.

I stayed on the bus, reading a book I'd carried just for this purpose. This didn't mean I had no worries, only that I'd learned not to let the fear start me running two hours before race time.

Little was at stake for me here. I'd run this far dozens of times before and had no time goal now. Still, I suffered from advanced anxiety.

In the last week before a race I expect every little twinge in my legs and tickle in my throat to magnify. The only treatment for these mostly imaginary ailments is to wait them out. They almost always pass, or at least lessen. Rarely does a problem that seemed so serious in recent days survive the first few minutes of a race.

TRAINING TIP

Treat the marathon as your graduation exercise. In those few hours, celebrate the good training that made this day possible. It's your reward for all the effort put in over the last few months.

Date _____ *Plans* _____

Training Session

Type of run □ long □ fast □ easy □ none □ race

Distance _____ *Time* _____

Pace _____ per mile _____ per kilometer

Splits _____ / _____ / _____ / _____ / _____ / _____

Effort □ max □ hard □ moderate □ easy □ rest

Training heart rates target _____ actual _____

Warm-up _____ *Cool-down* _____ *Cross-training* _____

Training Conditions

Location _____ *Time of day* _____

People □ alone □ with group □ race □ with partner _____
                                                            name

Surface □ road □ trail □ track □ mixed _____

Terrain □ flat □ hilly □ mixed _____

Weather _____ *Shoes worn* _____

Diet drinks during run _____ foods during run _____

Training Rating

Success level 10 9 8 7 6 5 4 3 2 1 0

Training Comments

_____

_____

_____

Necessary Worry

Early sleep the night before the Las Vegas Marathon didn't come as hoped. At bedtime I called home for messages. Son Eric answered with news that our dog, my running partner Mingo, had escaped and now had been gone for more than a day. We guessed that he was injured or worse. Sleep came grudgingly with Mingo's fate added to the usual marathon uncertainties.

At 2:30 I came awake with a strangely comforting thought: Mingo is either alive or not, and it's already decided. I can't do anything about it now. He reappeared later at the city pound, traumatized but otherwise okay.

Same with my run. Whether I finish it or not was already determined by what I'd done in training the past many weeks—and for my various aches and pains.

It was too late to change anything. All I could do now was go out and learn what the answers were. This attitude adopted, I fell into my best sleep of the night.

Worries came back with the predawn wakeup call, of course. But riding to the start with even more worried runners proved therapeutic.

About two days later, or so it seemed, the race started. My worries soon ended. The imagined ailments melted away in the first half-hour, leaving the normal challenges of a marathon.

I'm left hoping no cure is ever found for premarathon worries. They're a necessary part of the experience—the mind's way of getting the body ready for what lies ahead.

TRAINING TIP

Start your postrace celebration—along with your recovery—by eating soon after finishing. Carbohydrates fuel all those miles, and carbo reloading after a marathon helps you even more than loading up in advance.

Date _____ **Plans** _____

Training Session

Type of run   ☐ long   ☐ fast   ☐ easy   ☐ none   ☐ race

Distance _____   **Time** _____

Pace _____ per mile   _____ per kilometer

Splits _____ / _____ / _____ / _____ / _____ / _____

Effort   ☐ max   ☐ hard   ☐ moderate   ☐ easy   ☐ rest

Training heart rates   target _____   actual _____

Warm-up _____   **Cool-down** _____   **Cross-training** _____

Training Conditions

Location _____   **Time of day** _____

People   ☐ alone   ☐ with group   ☐ race   ☐ with partner _____

name

Surface   ☐ road   ☐ trail   ☐ track   ☐ mixed _____

Terrain   ☐ flat   ☐ hilly   ☐ mixed _____

Weather _____   **Shoes worn** _____

Diet   drinks during run _____   foods during run _____

Training Rating

Success level   10   9   8   7   6   5   4   3   2   1   0

Training Comments

_____

_____

_____

Your marathon doesn't end at the finish line. It isn't finished until you have recovered completely and can run normally.

EASING BACK

Recovering from a marathon takes longer than one week—and possibly more than a month. Recovery passes through several stages, and you barely finish the first of those this week. That's the sore-muscle stage, which peaks on the second day after the marathon and disappears by week's end. The more subtle effects remain. Fatigue lingers, along with a sense of psychological letdown that runners call *postmarathon blues.* These subtle effects take much longer to pass.

A popular rule of thumb states that the recovery period after a marathon lasts four to six weeks. What to do during that time? Run after the first few days, certainly. But keep the runs short and the pace easy; avoid all races. Don't schedule another marathon for yourself, or start training for one, until you satisfy all recovery requirements. Choose your program from the options listed, assign runs to the next seven days of diary pages, and add details there for completed training.

Cruiser Program

Big day: None.

Other training days: Three or four easy runs at whatever slow pace and short distance the legs allow.

Rest days: Three or four with no running, but possibly easy cross-training.

Pacer Program

Big day: None.

Other training days: Three or four easy runs at whatever slow pace and short distance the legs allow.

Rest days: Three or four days with no running, but possibly easy cross-training.

Racer Program

Long day: None.

Fast day: None.

Other training days: Three or four easy runs at whatever slow pace and short distance the legs allow.

Rest days: Three or four with no running, but possibly easy cross-training.

Afterthoughts

Two letter writers reminded me that not every marathoner yet knows of the lows that almost inevitably follow the highs of the event. The first e-mailed note, unsigned, came from a runner concerned about "slow" recovery from the Chicago Marathon.

"Nine days ago I ran my first marathon, an experience I really enjoyed," the note began. "Since then my aches and pains have left. However, I don't seem to have my energy back in spite of staying well hydrated and carbo reloading. What has surprised me the most is, I don't feel motivated to run like I used to."

A second correspondent, identifying herself only as Candy, wrote that her fall marathon had made her sick. "What can I do in my next marathon to keep from getting so run down for a month afterwards?" she asked. "After running Portland, I came down with the flu and took a long time to recover. I almost lost my love of running for about a month."

TRAINING TIP

Be prepared for postrace pain. You can expect stiffness in the thighs and calves, and you can wear your limp as a badge of courage. Rest until this soreness disappears, which should take less than a week.

The first runner's postmarathon reactions were textbook normal. Every symptom described is what we're supposed to feel for a few weeks after an accomplishment this big. We want to eat more, drink more, sleep more, and run less. Accept it as part of the experience.

I told the second marathoner that rundown-ness is the body and mind's way of protecting us against further damage. If we push too hard during the time when we should be taking it very easy, the body rebels with an injury or illness.

These maladies are common in the days and weeks after a marathon. They're the penalty for fighting the urge to be "lazy."

Date _____ **Plans** _____

Training Session

Type of run   ☐ long   ☐ fast   ☐ easy   ☐ none   ☐ race

Distance _____   **Time** _____

Pace _____ per mile   _____ per kilometer

Splits _____ / _____ / _____ / _____ / _____ / _____

Effort   ☐ max   ☐ hard   ☐ moderate   ☐ easy   ☐ rest

Training heart rates   target _____   actual _____

Warm-up _____   **Cool-down** _____   **Cross-training** _____

Training Conditions

Location _____   **Time of day** _____

People   ☐ alone   ☐ with group   ☐ race   ☐ with partner _____
                                                                    name

Surface   ☐ road   ☐ trail   ☐ track   ☐ mixed _____

Terrain   ☐ flat   ☐ hilly   ☐ mixed _____

Weather _____   **Shoes worn** _____

Diet   drinks during run _____   foods during run _____

Training Rating

Success level   10   9   8   7   6   5   4   3   2   1   0

Training Comments

_____

_____

_____

_____

Recovery Days

Allow at least one day per mile or per kilometer of the race for the doldrums to pass. That's four to six weeks after a marathon. During that time, don't even think about running anything hard.

A runner I'd introduced to this rule responded by asking for specifics: "How many easy miles should I be running each day during marathon recovery? I would hate to lose my fitness after all these months of training."

TRAINING TIP

While resting, leave the marathon time on your watch and glance at it proudly. As you start to run again, notice the zeroing of time. The marathon is finished, and you're starting over in training.

My practice, honed by dozens of marathons and many postmarathon mistakes, is to rest completely the next three or four days afterward. Then for the next week or so, run no longer than a half-hour. For the remainder of the following month, go no more than an hour—with no speed training or races. Little fitness is lost on such a routine, and it drastically cuts the risk of breakdowns.

Recovery goes through three stages, each taking longer than the one before. The first is recovery from acute muscle soreness, which takes no more than a few days to ease. Then you still have to deal with overall weariness, felt mostly as dead legs, which takes longer to wane. Finally there's psychological recovery, that don't-want-to-go-hard-again feeling that is slowest to leave you after a hard effort.

You know you're recovered fully when the legs feel pain-free and lively again. And when you've forgotten how hard the last race felt and want to try another.

Then, and only then, is when full training can resume. Only then do you plan your next marathon.

Date _____ *Plans* _____

Training Session

Type of run   □ long   □ fast   □ easy   □ none   □ race

Distance _____   *Time* _____

Pace _____ per mile   _____ per kilometer

Splits _____ / _____ / _____ / _____ / _____ / _____

Effort   □ max   □ hard   □ moderate   □ easy   □ rest

Training heart rates target _____   actual _____

Warm-up _____   *Cool-down* _____   *Cross-training* _____

Training Conditions

Location _____   *Time of day* _____

People □ alone   □ with group   □ race   □ with partner _____
                                                                name

Surface   □ road   □ trail   □ track   □ mixed _____

Terrain   □ flat   □ hilly   □ mixed _____

Weather _____   *Shoes worn* _____

Diet   drinks during run _____   foods during run _____

Training Rating

Success level   10   9   8   7   6   5   4   3   2   1   0

Training Comments

_____

_____

_____

Pacing Patiently

Distance running is one sport that requires doing less than your best most of the time. We talked about that in an earlier week, dealing with the importance of easy runs. You learn to hold back now so that you can keep going later.

Marathoning teaches many lessons. One of the best has to do with pacing. You can't run any early mile or kilometer of a long race all out, or you won't finish. Likewise, you can't train your hardest every day without ever easing off or resting, or you won't run regularly or for a long time.

TRAINING TIP

Resist the urge to rush back into full training as soon as your leg soreness eases. You've only passed through the most obvious but shortest stage of recovery. Two subtle and longer-lasting stages remain.

Running long distances requires that you pace yourself. Take that word *pace*, split it in half, add a few letters, and you have *patience*. That's what pacing is: an exercise in patience.

Walking to the start of the Portland Marathon one year, I happened to pass a church. Chiseled in concrete on one wall was the line, "Run with patience the race set before you." Someone more religious than I told me later that these words are Biblical, from Hebrews 12:1. All I knew at the time was how wisely they speak to runners, especially on marathon day.

A marathon demands patience, as gratification there is long delayed. The race doesn't start on race morning but months earlier with the decision to enter and the commitment to train.

You spend more of the training days holding back than pushing ahead. Then you reach race day and still must hold yourself back. Only in the shortest sprints do you run all-out from the first step onward. And you're no sprinter now.

Date _____ *Plans* _____

Training Session

Type of run ☐ long ☐ fast ☐ easy ☐ none ☐ race

Distance _____ **Time** _____

Pace _____ per mile _____ per kilometer

Splits _____ / _____ / _____ / _____ / _____ / _____

Effort ☐ max ☐ hard ☐ moderate ☐ easy ☐ rest

Training heart rates target _____ actual _____

Warm-up _____ **Cool-down** _____ **Cross-training** _____

Training Conditions

Location _____ **Time of day** _____

People ☐ alone ☐ with group ☐ race ☐ with partner _____
name

Surface ☐ road ☐ trail ☐ track ☐ mixed _____

Terrain ☐ flat ☐ hilly ☐ mixed _____

Weather _____ **Shoes worn** _____

Diet drinks during run _____ foods during run _____

Training Rating

Success level 10 9 8 7 6 5 4 3 2 1 0

Training Comments

_____

_____

_____

Waiting It Out

Even on marathon day the wait for your final reward is long, with many hours of running separating the start from the finish. The early miles feel too easy, but you restrain yourself then so that the late miles won't seem unbearably hard.

Even while pacing yourself well, you almost surely ran into what the British call "bad patches" in training and in the race itself. Your patience was put to its sternest test as you waded through and waited out the inevitable trouble spots—injuries, illnesses, crises of energy and confidence—that threatened to end your big effort too soon.

TRAINING TIP

Observe the second stage of recovery: the more hungry, thirsty, sleepy feeling. When you run, it's like you're wearing weighted boots. This stage takes several weeks to pass.

The lessons of pacing yourself patiently while training for and running in marathons carry over to the race of your life—the one with no finish line except the ultimate one. Here the right pace is one you can maintain indefinitely, through the good years and the not so good.

One year in a longtime runner's life is like a mile or kilometer in a marathon. You don't run the first one at a pace a minute or two faster than you expect to average. And you don't push the pace too hard in any season or year if you still expect to be running strongly next year or a decade or more down the road.

Either in races or in life, you can push hard for a short distance or back off for the long haul. Rare is the runner who can handle an intense pace for a long time.

Maybe you can't outrun the hard-paced runners today. But your chances are good of outlasting them in the long run if your pacing is more relaxed.

Date _____ **Plans** _____

Training Session

Type of run   □ long   □ fast   □ easy   □ none   □ race

Distance _____ **Time** _____

Pace _____ per mile   _____ per kilometer

Splits _____ / _____ / _____ / _____ / _____ / _____

Effort   □ max   □ hard   □ moderate   □ easy   □ rest

Training heart rates target _____ actual _____

Warm-up _____ **Cool-down** _____ **Cross-training** _____

Training Conditions

Location _____ **Time of day** _____

People □ alone □ with group □ race □ with partner _____
                                                                        name

Surface   □ road   □ trail   □ track   □ mixed _____

Terrain   □ flat   □ hilly   □ mixed _____

Weather _____ **Shoes worn** _____

Diet drinks during run _____ foods during run _____

Training Rating

Success level   10   9   8   7   6   5   4   3   2   1   0

Training Comments

_____

_____

_____

Peaceful Pace

I'm into my fifth decade as a runner. The length and pace of runs these days are nothing to shout about, but I take certain pride in the longevity because it isn't always easy to maintain.

The first two years of the 2000s tested my patience more than any similar period had before. Without going into the gory details, I first caught a long-lasting, strength-sapping illness. Finally recovered from that, I fell on a sidewalk and did slow-healing damage to a hip. Though my running never stopped for more than a week, the runs themselves were never shorter or slower.

TRAINING TIP

Observe the third stage of recovery: the psychological healing that often takes the longest. You can't think about running another marathon until you forget how hard the last one felt.

Here's where patience came into play. I couldn't rush recovery but had to hold back, do what was possible, and wait for better days ahead. Pace myself, in other words.

Taking a long-term view is most important during and right after a bad-patch period. The urge is to break through the trouble—to pick up the pace and make up for lost time. This is a time to stay within comfort-zone pace. Let progress come naturally instead of trying futilely to hurry it.

The waiting isn't as hard as it might sound, as long as you see hope for eventual recovery. One off day is an eye blink in the life of a runner; it's like a few steps in a marathon. One bad month is but a marathoner's minute; one year, less than a mile.

Taking the long view of pace gives you patience, and with patience comes peace of mind. Fittingly that word *peace* is in Italian spelled p-a-c-e.

Date _____ **Plans** _____

Training Session

Type of run ☐ long ☐ fast ☐ easy ☐ none ☐ race

Distance _____ **Time** _____

Pace _____ per mile _____ per kilometer

Splits _____ / _____ / _____ / _____ / _____ / _____

Effort ☐ max ☐ hard ☐ moderate ☐ easy ☐ rest

Training heart rates target _____ actual _____

Warm-up _____ **Cool-down** _____ **Cross-training** _____

Training Conditions

Location _____ **Time of day** _____

People ☐ alone ☐ with group ☐ race ☐ with partner _____
name

Surface ☐ road ☐ trail ☐ track ☐ mixed _____

Terrain ☐ flat ☐ hilly ☐ mixed _____

Weather _____ **Shoes worn** _____

Diet drinks during run _____ foods during run _____

Training Rating

Success level 10 9 8 7 6 5 4 3 2 1 0

Training Comments

_____

_____

_____

_____

Good Sport

I heard the same sentiments voiced twice within a half-hour at a race. The phrasings were different, and both would have been irritating or insulting if they hadn't been so off base.

A runner felt the need to say, "Your view of running is very different than mine. I think of it as an athletic event."

Mr. Serious implied that I don't know or care about the top end of the sport. My answer: You don't coauthor a 400-page book on the history of road racing (as I did with Rich Benyo for the *Running Encyclopedia*) without having some interest in the athletic side of running.

A reporter went even further by asking if running is athletic at all. "What is your response to people who say that it isn't really a sport?" he asked during an interview.

TRAINING TIP

Once the initial euphoria of finishing wears off, expect to encounter the postmarathon blues. This is a weariness of spirit, and the idea of running any distance at any pace doesn't excite you.

The question implied this: How can it be a sport if no ball or stick comes into play, or if it only employs a "skill" that we pretty well master by age two?

The two back-to-back questions set me to thinking about running as a sport. That was the only way I originally knew it. Before running also became a way to exercise, relax, or meditate, the only reason to run was to compete. Running was then and still is the purest of sports. You don't compete against an arbitrary standard like par for a course or points against an opponent. You compete with the most objective and inflexible of foes: time, distance, and yourself.

These aren't soft opponents. They challenge you to do your best and give you good ways to measure it.

Date _____ **Plans** _____

Training Session

Type of run   □ long   □ fast   □ easy   □ none   □ race

Distance _____ **Time** _____

Pace _____ per mile   _____ per kilometer

Splits _____ / _____ / _____ / _____ / _____ / _____

Effort   □ max   □ hard   □ moderate   □ easy   □ rest

Training heart rates target _____ actual _____

Warm-up _____ **Cool-down** _____ **Cross-training** _____

Training Conditions

Location _____ **Time of day** _____

People □ alone   □ with group   □ race   □ with partner _____
name

Surface   □ road   □ trail   □ track   □ mixed _____

Terrain   □ flat   □ hilly   □ mixed _____

Weather _____ **Shoes worn** _____

Diet drinks during run _____   foods during run _____

Training Rating

Success level   10   9   8   7   6   5   4   3   2   1   0

Training Comments

_____

_____

_____

Special Efforts

You can play in a sandlot softball game without practicing. You can shoot baskets without taking lessons. But you can't fake a running event. You can't go to the starting line with hopes of finishing in good shape and at your best pace without doing the training.

Almost anyone could train to run a race. But how many would? Great numbers of runners do it, you might think. The total count of finishers in American road races per year runs into the millions. About a quarter-million of those are marathoners.

The road racing population is large and growing larger each year. You might think that amid all these people your efforts shrink in value; you are just one more runner among hundreds of thousands. If you think that, you're reading the wrong numbers. Keep in mind that fewer than 1 in 10 Americans ever runs, and of the runners maybe 1 in 10 ever races, and of the racers only 1 in 10 ever finishes a marathon.

At the time I became a marathoner, we thought of ourselves as among the 1 in 100,000 Americans who could and would do this. The odds have decreased, but we're still oddities.

If you're among the quarter-million U.S. runners who finish marathons this year, that places you among the one-tenth of one percent of the country's population willing and able to run this far. This makes you pretty special. A sport that makes you feel that way is a true and good one.

You've found one. Now run with it as far and fast as you can go.

TRAINING TIP

Treat the postmarathon blues as a useful natural phenomenon that is both physical and psychological. You're still recovering, and your body and psyche aren't yet ready for a new goal as compelling as the last.

Date _____ **Plans** _____

Training Session

Type of run ☐ long ☐ fast ☐ easy ☐ none ☐ race

Distance _____ **Time** _____

Pace _____ per mile _____ per kilometer

Splits _____ / _____ / _____ / _____ / _____ / _____

Effort ☐ max ☐ hard ☐ moderate ☐ easy ☐ rest

Training heart rates target _____ actual _____

Warm-up _____ **Cool-down** _____ **Cross-training** _____

Training Conditions

Location _____ **Time of day** _____

People ☐ alone ☐ with group ☐ race ☐ with partner _____

name

Surface ☐ road ☐ trail ☐ track ☐ mixed _____

Terrain ☐ flat ☐ hilly ☐ mixed _____

Weather _____ **Shoes worn** _____

Diet drinks during run _____ foods during run _____

Training Rating

Success level 10 9 8 7 6 5 4 3 2 1 0

Training Comments

_____

_____

_____

PICKING
YOUR MARATHON

Where to run your next marathon? Your choices number in the hundreds, and this without even leaving the North American continent. *Runner's World* magazine lists more than 300 races each year in the United States and Canada. They occur on nearly every weekend of any year.

Following is a wide selection of U.S. and Canadian marathons, with one or more per state and province. Included are the biggest and best-known events, the oldest that date from at least the early 1970s (indicated with *), and many I've run or visited (indicated with +).

Information includes name of the marathon, location, usual month of its running, a phone number, Web site, and address as of the event's 2003 running. Check each January *Runner's World* and www.runnersworld.com (or the independent www.marathonguide.com) for updates.

UNITED STATES

Alabama

Mercedes Marathon, Birmingham (February): 2839 18th St. S., Birmingham, AL 35209; 205-870-5644; www.mercedesmarathon.com

Rocket City Marathon, Huntsville (December): 1101 Opp Reynolds Rd., Toney, AL 35773; 256-828-6207; www.huntsvilletrackclub.org

Alaska

* Equinox Marathon, Fairbanks (September): Box 84237, Fairbanks, AK 99708; 907-452-8351; www.equinoxmarathon.org

Mayor's Midnight Sun Marathon, Anchorage (June): Box 196650, Anchorage, AK 99519; 907-343-4296; www.mayorsmarathon.com

+ Prince of Wales International Marathon, Craig (May): Box 497, Craig, AK 99921; 907-826-3870; www.powmarathon.org

Arizona

Rock 'n' Roll Arizona Marathon, Phoenix (January): 5452 Oberlin Dr. Ste. B, San Diego, CA 92121; 858-450-6510; www.eliteracing.com

* Tucson Marathon (December): Box 64938, Tucson, AZ 85712; 520-320-0667; www.tucsonmarathon.com

Arkansas

Arkansas Marathon, Malvern (October): 1200 Clardy St., Malvern, AR 72104; 870-540-3174; www.arkansasrunner.com

Hogeye Marathon, Fayetteville (March): 646 Robin Hood Ct., Springdale, AK 72764; 479-575-2975; www.hogeyemarathon.org

California

*+ Avenue of the Giants Marathon, Weott (May): 81 Hidden Valley Rd., Bayside, CA 95524; 707-443-1226; www.theave.org

+ Big Sur International Marathon, Carmel (April): Box 222620, Carmel, CA 93922; 831-625-6226; www.bsim.org

California International Marathon, Sacramento (December): Box 161149, Sacramento, CA 95816; 916-983-4622; www.runcim.org

+ Chronicle Marathon, San Francisco (July): Box 828, Rialto, CA 92377; 800-698-8699; www.chroniclemarathon.com

+ Long Beach International Marathon (October): 555 E. Artesia Blvd. Ste. B, Long Beach, CA 90805; 562-728-8829; www.runlongbeach.com

+ Los Angeles Marathon (March): 11110 W. Ohio Ave. No. 100, Los Angeles, CA 90025; 310-444-5544; www.lamarathon.com

+ Napa Valley Marathon, Napa (March): Box 4307, Napa, CA 94558; 707-255-2609; www.napa-marathon.com

* Palos Verdes Marathon (May): 1666 Ashland Ave., Santa Monica, CA 90405; 310-828-4123; www.w2promo.com

Rock 'n' Roll Marathon, San Diego (June): 5452 Oberlin Dr. Ste. B, San Diego, CA 92121; 858-450-6510; www.rnrmarathon.com

*+ San Diego Marathon (January): 511 S. Cedros Ave., Solana Beach, CA 92075; 858-792-2900; www.sdmarathon.com

*+ Western Hemisphere Marathon, Culver City (December): 1129 Cardiff Ave., Los Angeles, CA 90035; 310-246-1418; www.whmarathon.active.com

Colorado

* Mile-High City Marathon (September): Box 40065, Denver, CO 80204; 303-375-8121; www.milehighcitymarathon.com

*+ Pike's Peak Marathon, Manitou Springs (August): Box 38235, Colorado Springs, CO 80937; 719-473-2625; www.pikespeakmarathon.org

+ Steamboat Marathon, Steamboat Springs (June): Box 774408, Steamboat Springs, CO 80477; 970-879-0880; www.steamboat-chamber.com

Connecticut

Greater Hartford Marathon (October): 119 Hebron Ave., Glastonbury, CT 06033; 860-652-8866; www.hartfordmarathon.com

Mystic Places Marathon, East Lyme (October): 2 Buena Vista Rd., Branford, CT 06405; 203-481-5933; www.mysticplacesmarathon.com

Delaware

Delaware Marathon, Dewey Beach (November): Box 24, Montchanin, DE 19710; 302-654-6400; www.places2run.com

Trail Triple Crown Marathon, Newark (April): 711 Fiske Ln., Newark, DE 19711; 302-453-0859; www.traildawgs.org/tc

District of Columbia

+ Marine Corps Marathon, Washington (October): Box 188, Quantico, VA 22134; 703-784-2225; www.marinemarathon.com

Washington Marathon (March): Box 17051, Arlington, VA 22221; 703-528-8176; www.washingtondcmarathon.com

Florida

Miami Tropical Marathon (February): Box 56-1081, Miami, FL 33256; 305-278-8668; www.miamitropical.com

Walt Disney World Marathon, Orlando (January): Box 536547, Orlando, FL 32853; 407-896-1160; www.disneyworldsports.com

Georgia

* Atlanta Marathon (November): 3097 E. Shadowlawn Ave., Atlanta, GA 30305; 404-231-0965; www.atlantatrackclub.org

Callaway Gardens Marathon, Marietta (February): 1930 Beaver Brook Ln., Marietta, GA 30062; 770-565-5208; www.callawaygardens.com/events/marathon

Hawaii

*+ Honolulu Marathon (December): 3435 Waialae Ave. No. 208, Honolulu, HI 96816; 808-734-7200; www.honolulumarathon.org

*+ Maui Marathon, Kahului (September): Box 330099, Kahului, HI 96733; 808-871-6441; www.mauimarathon.com

Idaho

+ City of Trees Marathon, Boise (November): 1414 W. Franklin St., Boise, ID 83702; 208-395-1900; www.cityoftreesmarathon.com

Coeur d'Alene Marathon (May): Box 3156, Coeur d'Alene, ID 83816; 208-665-9393; www.cdamarathon.org

Illinois

+ Chicago Marathon (October): Box 10597, Chicago, IL 60610; 312-904-9800; www.chicagomarathon.com

Quad Cities Marathon, Moline, IL (September): 920 15th Ave., Moline, IL 61244; 309-751-9800; www.qcmarathon.org

Indiana

Indianapolis Marathon (October): Box 36214, Indianapolis, IN 46236; 317-826-1670; www.indianapolismarathon.com

Sunburst Marathon, South Bend (June): 111 W. Jefferson Blvd. Ste. 300, South Bend, IN 46601; 574-284-3394; no Web site listed.

Iowa

Des Moines Marathon (October): 201 Locust St. No. 239, Des Moines, IA 50309; 515-288-2692; www.desmoinesmarathon.com

University of Okoboji Marathon, Pike's Point State Park (July): Box 7933, Spencer, IA 51301; 712-338-2424; www.okoboji.com

Kansas

Eisenhower Marathon, Abilene (March): 206 N. Broadway, Abilene, KS 6740; 785-263-2341; www.dickinsoncounty.redcross.org

Wichita Marathon (October): Box 782050, Wichita, KS 67278; 316-708-0808; www.runwichita.org

Kentucky

Kentucky Derby Marathon, Louisville (April): Box 35273, Louisville, KY 40232; 502-584-6383; www.mini.derbyfestival.com/marathon

Louisville Marathon (October): 1198 Ampere Ct., Louisville, KY 40299; 502-267-1825; www.louisvillemarathon.org

Louisiana

Baton Rouge Beach Marathon (November): 3214 Kings Mountain, Kingwood, TX 77345; 281-913-1841; www.brbmarathon.com

*+ Mardi Gras Marathon, New Orleans (February): Box 8788, Metarie, LA 70011; 504-454-8687; www.mardigrasmarathon.com

Maine

Maine Marathon, Portland (October): Box 10836, Portland, ME 04104; 207-741-2084; www.mainmarathon.com

Sugarloaf Marathon, Eustis (May): RR 1 Box 5000, Carrabassett Valley, ME 04947; 207-237-6830; no Web site listed.

Maryland

Baltimore Marathon (October): 201 W. Baltimore St., Baltimore, MD 21201; 410-605-9381; www.thebaltimoremarathon.com

* Washington's Birthday Marathon, Greenbelt (February): Box 1352, Arlington, VA 22210; 703-241-0395; www.dcroadrunners.org/gwmarathon

Massachusetts

* Bay State Marathon, Tyngsboro (October): 22 Winsor Dr., Dracut, MA 01826; 978-957-6447; www.baystatemarathon.com

*+ Boston Athletic Association Marathon (April): 1 Ash St., Hopkinton, MA 01748; 508-435-6905; www.bostonmarathon.org

*Race of Champions Marathon, Holyoke (May): 231 E. Elm St., West Springfield, MA 01089; 413-734-0955; www.harriers.org

Michigan

Bayshore Marathon, Traverse City (May): Box 4026, Traverse City, MI 49685; 231-941-8118; www.bayshoremarathon.org

*+ Detroit International Marathon, Detroit (October): 600 W. Fort St., Detroit, MI 48226; 313-222-6676; www.freep.com/marathon

Minnesota

Grandma's Marathon, Duluth (June): Box 16234, Duluth, MN 55816; 218-727-0947; www.grandmasmarathon.com

*+ Twin Cities Marathon, Minneapolis-St. Paul (October): 708 N. First St., Minneapolis, MN 55401; 612-925-3500; www.twincitiesmarathon.org

+ Walker North Country Marathon, Walker (September): Box 1440, Walker, MN 56484; 218-547-3327; www.active.com

Mississippi

Mississippi Marathon, Clinton (January): Box 1414, Ridgeland, MS 39157; 601-856-9884; www.mstrackclub.com

Tupelo Marathon (September): 2411 Crestwood Dr., Tupelo, MS 38801; 662-842-8958; www.tupelorunningclub.homestead.com

Missouri

* Heart of America Marathon, Columbia (September): 2605 Chapel Wood Terr., Columbia, MO 65203; 573-445-2684; www.ctc.coin.org/hoa

+ Humana River Crown Plaza Marathon, Kansas City (November): Box 1216, Raymore, MO 64083; 816-331-4286; www.humanamarathon.com

+ Spirit of St. Louis Marathon, St. Louis (April): 214 S. Bemiston Ste. 2N, Clayton, MO 63105; 314-727-0800; www.stlouismarathon.com

Montana

Governor's Cup Marathon, Helena (June): Box 451, Helena, MT 59624; 406-447-3414; www.govcup.bcbsmt.com

Lewis & Clark Marathon, Bozeman (August): 1627 W. Main St. No. 306, Bozeman, MT 59715; 406-556-9736; www.lewisandclarkmarathon.com

Nebraska

+ Lincoln Marathon (May): 882 N. Lakeshore Dr., Lincoln, NE 68528; 402-435-3504; www.lincolnrun.org

Omaha Marathon (September): Box 241811, Omaha, NE 68124; 402-354-1000; www.omahamarathon.com

Nevada

*+ Las Vegas International Marathon (February): Box 81262, Las Vegas, NV 89180; 702-240-2722; www.lvmarathon.com

Silver State Marathon, Reno (August): Box 21171, Reno, NV 89515; 775-851-8369; www.silverstatemarathon.com

New Hampshire

Clarence DeMar Marathon, Gilsum (September): Box 1757, Keene, NH 03431; 603-358-4114; www.clarencedemar.com

New Hampshire Marathon, Bristol (October): Box 6, Bristol, NH 03222; 603-744-2150; www.newfoundchamber.com

New Jersey

* Atlantic City Marathon (October): Box 2181, Ventnor, NJ 08406; 609-601-1786; www.racegate.com

* New Jersey Shore Marathon (April): Box 198, Oceanport, NJ 07757; 731-578-1771; www.njshoremarathon.org

New Mexico

* Duke City Marathon, Albuquerque (September): 6565 America's Parkway N.E., Albuquerque, NM 87110; 505-880-1414; www.dukecitymarathon.com

Shiprock Marathon, Farmington, NM (May): Box 1676, Farmington, NM 87499; 505-368-3511; www.shiprock.dinecollege.edu/srmarathon

New York

* Long Island Marathon, East Meadow (May): Sports Unit, Hempstead Turnpike, Eisenhower Park, East Meadow, NY 11554; 516-572-0251; no Web site listed.

*+ New York City Marathon (November): Box 1388 GPO, New York, NY 10116; 212-423-2249; www.nycmarathon.org

+ Wineglass Marathon, Corning (October): Box 117, Corning, NY 14830; 607-936-4686; www.wineglassmarathon.com

* Yonkers Marathon (September): 285 Nepperhan Ave., Yonkers, NY 10701; 914-377-6430; www.cityofyonkers.com/parks/marathon

North Carolina

+ Charlotte Observer Marathon, Charlotte (January): 2910 Selwyn Ave. No. 326, Charlotte, NC 28209; 704-333-3688; www.runforpeace.active.com

* Grandfather Mountain Marathon, Boone (July): 156 Olancha Ave., Boone, NC 28607; 828-264-8861; www.grandfatherbear.com

* Raleigh Marathon (December): Box 2626, Raleigh, NC 27602; 919-266-2444; www.raleighmarathon.com

North Dakota

Bismarck YMCA Marathon (September): Box 549, Bismarck, ND 58502; 701-255-1525; no Web site listed.

Trestle Valley Marathon, Minot (April): Box 69, Minot, ND 58702; 701-852-0141; www.ymcaminot.org/special

Ohio

* Athens Marathon (April): 7154 Radford Rd., Athens, OH 45701; 740-594-3825; www.athensmarathon.org

Cleveland Marathon (April): 2525 Chagrin Blvd. No. 316, Pepper Pike, OH 44122; 800-467-3826; www.clevelandmarathon.com

+ Columbus Marathon (October): 833 Eastwind Dr., Westerville, OH 43081; 614-794-1566; www.columbusmarathon.com

Flying Pig Marathon, Cincinnati (May): 644 Linn St. No. 626, Cincinnati, OH 45203; 513-721-7447; www.flyingpigmarathon.com

*+ Glass City Marathon, Toledo (April): 130 Yale, Toledo, OH 43614; 419-385-7025; www.toledoroadrunners.org

* Ohio River RRC Marathon, Dayton (April): Box 2332, Dayton, OH 45420; 937-297-0650; www.orrrc.org/marathon

Oklahoma

* Andy Payne Marathon, Oklahoma City (May): Box 800, Oklahoma City, OK 73101; 405-236-2800; www.unityinc.org

+ Oklahoma City Memorial Marathon (April): 53 N.W. 42nd, Oklahoma City, OK 73118; 405-525-4242; www.okcmarathon.com

Oregon

+ Newport Marathon (June): 1215 N.E. Lakewood Dr., Newport, OR 97365; 541-265-3446; www.newportmarathon.org

*+ Portland Marathon (October): Box 4040, Beaverton, OR 97076; 503-226-1111; www.portlandmarathon.org

Pennsylvania

+ City of Pittsburgh Marathon (May): 200 Lothrop St., Pittsburgh, PA 15213; 412-647-7866; www.upmc.edu/pghmarathon

* Philadelphia Marathon (November): Box 21601, Philadelphia, PA 19131; 215-685-0054; www.philadelphiamarathon.com

Rhode Island

Ocean State Marathon, Warwick (October): 5 Division St., East Greenwich, RI 02818; 401-885-4499; www.osm26.com

South Carolina

Kiawah Island Marathon (December): 12 Kiawah Beach Dr., Kiawah Island, SC 29455; 843-768-2780; www.kiawahresort.com/marathon

Myrtle Beach Marathon (February): Box 8780, Myrtle Beach, SC 29578; 843-293-7223; www.mbmarathon.com

South Dakota

* Longest Day Marathon, Brookings (April): Box 8012, Brookings, SD 57006; 605-696-1358; www.prairiestriders.net

Mount Rushmore Marathon, Rapid City (October): Box 747, Rapid City, SD 57709; 800-487-3223; www.mountrushmoremarathon.com

Tennessee

* Andrew Jackson Marathon, Jackson, TN (April): 60 Rolling Hills Dr., Jackson, TN 38305; 901-668-1708; www.jacksonroadrunners.org

Country Music Marathon, Nashville (April): 240 Great Circle Rd. No. 340, Nashville, TN 37228; 800-311-1255; www.cmmarathon.com

Texas

+ Cowtown Marathon, Fort Worth (February): Box 9066, Fort Worth, TX 76147; 817-735-2033; www.cowtownmarathon.org

*+ Dallas White Rock Marathon (December):8189 South Central Expressway, Dallas, TX 75241; 214-372-2068; www.runtherock.com

+ HP Houston Marathon (January): 720 Post Oak Rd. No. 100, Houston, TX 77024; 713-957-3453; www.hphoustonmarathon.com

Motorola Marathon, Austin (February): Box 684587, Austin, TX 78768; 877-601-6686; www.motorolamarathon.com

Utah

*+ Deseret News Marathon, Salt Lake City (July): 30 E. 100 S., Salt Lake City, UT 84111; 801-237-2135; www.deseretnews.com/run

St. George Marathon (October): 86 S. Main St., St. George, UT 84770; 435-634-5850; www.stgeorgemarathon.com

Vermont

Green Mountain Marathon, South Hero (October): Box 527, Richmond, VT 05477; 802-434-3228; no Web site listed.

Vermont City Marathon, Burlington (May): 1 Main St. No. 304, Burlington, VT 05401; 802-863-8412; www.vcm.org

Virginia

Shamrock Marathon, Virginia Beach (March): 2321 Cape Arbor Dr., Virginia Beach, VA 23451; 757-496-51832; www.shamroacksportsfest.com

Trigon Bay Bridge Marathon, Virginia Beach (October): 265 King's Grant Rd., Virginia Beach, VA 23452; 757-498-0215; www.baybridgemarathon.com

Washington

* Birch Bay Marathon, Blaine (December): 1841 Dike Road, Mount Vernon, WA 98273; 360-848-1146; no Web site listed.

+ Capital City Marathon, Olympia (May): Box 1681, Olympia, WA 98507; 360-786-1786; www.ontherun.com/cma

* Seattle Marathon (November): Box 31849, Seattle, WA 98103; 206-729-3660; www.seattlemarathon.org

* Spokane Marathon (October): 605 W. Bradford Ct., Spokane, WA 99203; 509-624-4297; www.ontherun.com

+ Yakima River Canyon Marathon, Selah (April): 10519 122th Ave. S.E., Renton, WA 98056; 425-226-1518; www.ontherun.com/yrcm

West Virginia

Hatfield-McCoy Marathon, Williamson (June): 801 Mudlick Rd., Hardy, WV 41531; 606-353-1626; www.hatfieldmccoymarathon.com

Ridge Runner Marathon, Cairo (June): Rt. 1 Box 221, Cairo, WV 26337; 304-643-2931; no Web site listed.

Wisconsin

Fox Cities Marathon, Neenah (September): Box 1315, Appleton, WI 54912; 920-882-9499; www.foxcitiesmarathon.org

Lakefront Marathon, Milwaukee (October): 9200 W. North Ave., Milwaukee, WI 53226; 414-291-2647; www.badgerlandstriders.org/lakefront

* Paavo Nurmi Marathon, Hurley (August): 316 Silver St., Hurley, WI 54534; 715-561-3290; www.hurleywi.com

Wyoming

Casper Wyoming Marathon (June): Box 1152, Casper, WY 82602; 307-261-6543; www.runwyoming.com

Wyoming Marathon, Laramie (May): 402 W. 31st St., Cheyenne, WY 82001; 307-635-3316; www.angelfire.com/wy2/marathon

CANADA

Alberta

*+ Calgary Stampede Marathon (July): Box 296 Station M, Calgary, AB T2P 2H9; 403-264-2996; www.stampederoadrace.com

+ Edmonton Festival Marathon (June): 8537 109th St., Edmonton, AB T6G 1E4; 780-433-6062; www.runningroom.com

+ Oil Sands Marathon, Fort McMurray (September): Box 5792, Fort McMurray, AB T9H 4V9; 780-743-1609; www.fmc.ab.ca

British Columbia

+ Okanagan International Marathon, Kelowna (October): 115-2463 Hwy. 97 N., Kelowna, BC V1X 4S2; 250-862-3511; www.runningroom.ca

+ Peach City Marathon, Penticton (May): 11-212 Main St., Penticton, BC V2A 2S9; 250-490-3334; www.peachcityrunners.com

+ Royal Victoria Marathon (October): 182-911 Yates St., Victoria, BC V8V 4X3; 250-382-8181; www.royalvictoriamarathon.com

*+ Vancouver International Marathon (May): Box 3213, Vancouver, BC V6B 3X8; 604-872-2928; www.adidasvanmarathon.ca

Manitoba

*+ Manitoba Marathon (June): 200 Main St., Winnipeg, MB R3C 4M2; 204-925-5751; www.manitobamarathon.mb.ca

New Brunswick

Fredericton Marathon (May): Box 1253, Fredericton, NB E38 5CB; 506-454-8880; www.canadiansport.net/ccrr

Marathon by the Sea Marathon, St. John (August): 50 Union St., St. John, NB E2L 1A1; 506-658-4715; www.marathonbythesea.com

Northwest Territories

Yellowknife Marathon (August): Box 191, Yellowknife, NWT X1A 2N2; 867-766-3422; www.ykmultipsport.com

Nova Scotia

Johnny Miles Marathon, New Glasgow (June): Box 426, New Glasgow, NS B2H 5E5; 902-7555-5537; no Web site listed.

Lake Ainslie Marathon (September): 2964 Route 395, East Lake Ainslie, NS B0E 3M0; 902-258-2097; www.users.auracom.com/lamarathon

Ontario

Canadian International Marathon, Toronto (October): 240 Heath St. W. No. 802, Toronto, ON M5P 3L5; 416-972-1068; www.runtoronto.com

Casino Niagara Marathon, Niagara Falls (October): 5515 Stanley Ave., Niagara Falls, ON L2G 3X4; 905-356-6061; www.niagarafallstourism.com

+ National Capital Marathon, Ottawa (May): Box 426 Station A, Ottawa, ON K1N 8V5; 613-234-2221; www.ncm.ca

Quebec

Quebec City Marathon (August): 1173 Boul. Charest Ouest Bureau 290, Quebec, QB G1N 2C; 418-694-4442; www.marathonquebec.com

Saskatchewan

Saskatchewan Marathon, Saskatoon (September): 704 Broadway Ave., Saskatoon, SK S7M 1B4; 306-244-0955; www.saskatoonroadrunners.ca

Yukon

Mayo Midnight Marathon (June): Box 152, Mayo, YK Y0B 1M0; 867-996-2368; www.users.yknet.yk.ca/mayomidnightmarathon

Yukon River Trail Marathon, Whitehorse (August): 201B Main St., Whitehorse, YK Y1A 2B2; 867-668-2858; www.yukonmarathon.com

PREDICTING YOUR TIME

You can forecast your time for a marathon even if you haven't run one before, or recently. Runners typically slow down by 5 percent or so per mile or kilometer as the distance doubles. The following figures are derived from multiplying the most recent half-marathon time by 2.3 (for Cruisers), 2.2 (for Pacers), and 2.1 (for Racers).

Half-marathon time	Cruisers prediction	Pacers prediction	Racers prediction
1:10:00	2:41:00	2:34:00	2:27:00
1:15:00	2:53:00	2:45:00	2:38:00
1:20:00	3:04:00	2:56:00	2:48:00
1:25:00	3:16:00	3:07:00	2:59:00
1:30:00	3:27:00	3:18:00	3:09:00
1:35:00	3:39:00	3:29:00	3:20:00
1:40:00	3:50:00	3:40:00	3:30:00
1:45:00	4:02:00	3:51:00	3:41:00
1:50:00	4:13:00	4:02:00	3:51:00
1:55:00	4:25:00	4:13:00	4:02:00
2:00:00	4:36:00	4:24:00	4:12:00
2:05:00	4:48:00	4:35:00	4:23:00
2:10:00	4:59:00	4:46:00	4:33:00
2:15:00	5:11:00	4:57:00	4:44:00
2:20:00	5:22:00	5:08:00	4:54:00
2:25:00	5:34:00	5:19:00	5:05:00
2:30:00	5:45:00	5:30:00	5:15:00
2:35:00	5:57:00	5:41:00	5:26:00
2:40:00	6:08:00	5:52:00	5:36:00
2:45:00	6:20:00	6:03:00	5:47:00

PACING YOUR MARATHON

Running a marathon is an exercise in restraint. A successful finish demands a cautious start. This table lists the desired splits at 5-kilometer and 5-mile checkpoints as well as at the halfway mark. The ranges of times are based on even pace, minus or plus five seconds per mile (three seconds per kilometer). Realistically predict your final time, then plan to start no faster or slower than indicated here.

Marathon goal (per mile/per K)	5K splits	5M splits	Half-marathon
2:20:00 (5:21/3:19)	16:25 to 16:40	26:35 to 27:00	1:09:00 to 1:11:00
2:30:00 (5:44/3:33)	17:40 to 17:55	28:25 to 28:50	1:14:00 to 1:16:00
2:40:00 (6:06/3:47)	18:50 to 19:05	30:20 to 30:45	1:19:00 to 1:21:00
2:50:00 (6:29/4:02)	20:00 to 20:15	32:15 to 32:40	1:24:00 to 1:26:00
3:00:00 (6:52/4:16)	21:10 to 21:25	34:10 to 34:35	1:29:00 to 1:31:00
3:10:00 (7:15/4:30)	22:25 to 22:40	36:05 to 36:30	1:34:00 to 1:36:00
3:20:00 (7:38/4:44)	23:35 to 23:50	37:55 to 38:20	1:39:00 to 1:41:00
3:30:00 (8:01/4:58)	24:45 to 25:00	39:50 to 40:15	1:44:00 to 1:46:00
3:40:00 (8:24/5:12)	25:55 to 26:10	41:45 to 42:10	1:49:00 to 1:51:00
3:50:00 (8:47/5:27)	27:05 to 27:20	43:40 to 44:05	1:54:00 to 1:56:00
4:00:00 (9:09/5:41)	28:20 to 28:35	45:35 to 46:00	1:59:00 to 2:01:00
4:10:00 (9:32/5:55)	29:30 to 29:45	47:30 to 47:55	2:04:00 to 2:06:00
4:20:00 (9:55/6:10)	30:40 to 30:55	49:25 to 49:50	2:09:00 to 2:11:00
4:30:00 (10:18/6:24)	31:50 to 32:15	51:20 to 51:45	2:14:00 to 2:16:00
4:40:00 (10:41/6:38)	33:00 to 33:25	53:10 to 53:35	2:19:00 to 2:21:00
4:50:00 (11:04/6:52)	34:15 to 34:30	55:05 to 55:30	2:24:00 to 2:26:00
5:00:00 (11:27/7:06)	35:25 to 35:40	57:05 to 57:30	2:29:00 to 2:31:00
5:10:00 (11:50/7:21)	36:35 to 36:50	59:00 to 59:25	2:34:00 to 2:36:00
5:20:00 (12:12/7:35)	37:45 to 38:00	60:55 to 61:20	2:39:00 to 2:41:00
5:30:00 (12:36/7:49)	39:00 to 39:15	62:50 to 63:15	2:44:00 to 2:46:00
5:40:00 (12:58/8:03)	40:10 to 40:25	64:45 to 65:10	2:49:00 to 2:51:00
5:50:00 (13:21/8:18)	41:20 to 41:35	66:40 to 67:05	2:54:00 to 2:56:00
6:00:00 (13:45/8:32)	42:30 to 42:45	68:35 to 69:00	2:59:00 to 3:01:00

INDEX

ABOUT THE AUTHOR

Joe Henderson has been writing about running for more than 40 years. He's the West Coast editor for *Runner's World* magazine and the author of more than 20 books on running, including several by Human Kinetics: *Better Runs, Running 101,* and *Fitness Running.* He is a columnist with *Runner's World,* publishes the newsletter *Running Commentary,* and teaches running courses at the University of Oregon.

The Road Runners Club of America has twice named Henderson Journalist of the Year. He is also a member of the club's Hall of Fame. He lives in Eugene, Oregon, with his wife, Barbara Shaw.

BOOKS BY JOE HENDERSON

Long Slow Distance
Road Racers and Their Training
Thoughts on the Run
Run Gently, Run Long
The Long Run Solution
Jog Run Race
Run Farther, Run Faster
The Running Revolution
Running A to Z
Running Your Best Race
Running for Fitness, for Sport and for Life
Joe Henderson's Running Handbook
Total Fitness
Think Fast
Masters Running and Racing (with Bill Rodgers and Priscilla Welch)
Fitness Running (with Richard Brown)
Did I Win?
Better Runs
Road Racers and Their Training, Second Edition
Marathon Training
Coaching Cross-Country Successfully (with Joe Newton)
Best Runs
Running 101
Running Encyclopedia (with Richard Benyo)
Fitness Running, Second Edition (with Richard Brown)
Marathon Training, Second Edition